Core Knowledge®

ISBN: 978-1-68380-328-7

The Enlightenment

Table of Contents

Reader
Core Knowledge History and Geography™

Chapter 1
Isaac Newton

Into the Light Imagine yourself in a dark room. You can't see anything—not even your hand in front of your face. Then, someone lights a candle. At first, you see only shapes and shadows. Then, a second candle is lit, followed by a third candle, and a fourth.

The Big Question

What part did scientific observation and reason play in Isaac Newton's thought process, and why did he hesitate to publish his findings?

As the glow of light brightens the room, the darkness gradually turns to light. How grateful you are for the candles that brought this "enlightenment."

Nowadays when the term *Enlightenment* is used, it does not refer to lighting candles, but to a period in history in Europe in the 1600s and 1700s. During that time, people all over Europe, and then throughout their colonies, believed that the darkness of the past was giving way to light. The darkness was ignorance, superstition, and unproven beliefs; the light was knowledge and the improvement it brought.

Vocabulary

reason, n. the ability of the mind to think clearly and understand; logic

What "candle" brought this new light? It was **reason**, or people's unique ability to question, analyze, and reach conclusions based on their own experience, and not on what some other authority said.

John Locke (1632–1704)

The Enlightenment is viewed as a time in history when certain people shed light on new ways of thinking.

John Locke (1632–1704), an English thinker of this period (you will read about him later), described reason as "the candle in men's minds . . . [that] must be our last judge and guide in everything."

The Renaissance paved the way for the Enlightenment. While Renaissance thinkers turned to ancient Greece and Rome for inspiration, educated Europeans of the 1600s and 1700s turned to reason and history. They said we no longer had to guess about the universe or accept the beliefs of ancient authorities. Instead, human beings, with reason and experience as their guides, could uncover the laws of nature and even come to understand the basic principles of human society and government.

The Enlightenment, also called the Age of Reason, changed history by creating the beginnings of the modern world we live in today. It brought revolutions in philosophy, science, mathematics, and government. It led to practical improvements that made the world a better place to live.

Setting the Scene

Let's look at Western Europe in the early 1600s, on the eve of the Enlightenment. For a small group of upper-class people, those people at the top of this society, home was a palace or manor. Within the grand houses, every object—each candlestick, every knife, fork, and spoon—was a work of art. The lords and ladies of this elite group dressed in lace and silk. Kings believed in the "**divine right of kings**"—the belief that a monarch's right to the throne was granted by God, and that rebellion against them was a sin. In this world, everyone was obedient to the king. The king did as he pleased.

> **Vocabulary**
>
> **"divine right of kings,"** (phrase) the belief that kings and queens have a God-given right to rule, and that rebellion against them is a sin

Life was very different for the lower groups or classes: the peasants, the workers, and the soldiers. For these people, life was hard. Many city dwellers lived in crowded neighborhoods. Peasants worked from dawn to dusk but owned very little. Fewer than half the babies born during this time reached adulthood. Few people lived to old age. Many were poor. Prisons were often full. Most common people had few rights or freedoms.

But a new group of people was rising, neither as rich as the nobles nor as poor as the peasants. Those who belonged to this middle group—or middle class—were destined to be the leaders of the Enlightenment. As towns and cities grew during this time, merchants, bankers, traders, and skilled craftspeople thrived.

Some grew rich and lived much like the lords and ladies who surrounded the monarchs. The members of this new middle class were called "burghers" (/ber*gerz/), because they mostly lived in burgs, or towns. Today, we still call the middle class the *bourgeois* (/boor*jwah/), from the French word meaning town dweller.

The rising middle class had money to spare. Not only could they buy luxury items, they could also invest their money in pursuits that were of interest to them, like reading and socializing in clubs.

Isaac Newton

Into this setting entered one of the greatest scientists in history: a man who changed the world forever. His name was Isaac Newton (1642–1727). Newton was born in England on Christmas Day, 1642. Young Isaac was a tiny baby, described as so small he could "fit into a quart pot." But this tiny baby grew to become an intellectual giant. Isaac Newton discovered the laws of **gravitation** and motion, invented a new branch of mathematics called **calculus**, and revealed the secrets of light and color—all within an eighteen-month period.

How did he do it? Like any person today, Newton relied on his ability to observe things and to think about what he observed. But unlike most people, Newton was actually a genius. In later life, he wrote, "I seem to have been only like a boy playing on the seashore . . . now and then finding a smoother pebble or a prettier shell than ordinary, whilst the great ocean of truth lay all undiscovered before me." The idea that truth is like a great ocean waiting to be discovered was one of the central ideas of the Enlightenment. In this regard, Newton followed in the footsteps of his countryman, Sir Francis Bacon (1561–1626).

In the early 1600s, Bacon had argued that when scientists look at the world around them, they should not always accept what past scientists thought to be true. Instead, they should use their senses to make observations and conduct experiments. By doing so, scientists would improve their knowledge and understanding of the world. He also thought that this gained knowledge of the natural world would give people the power to make better lives. Others were thinking similar thoughts. In 1660, some of them came together

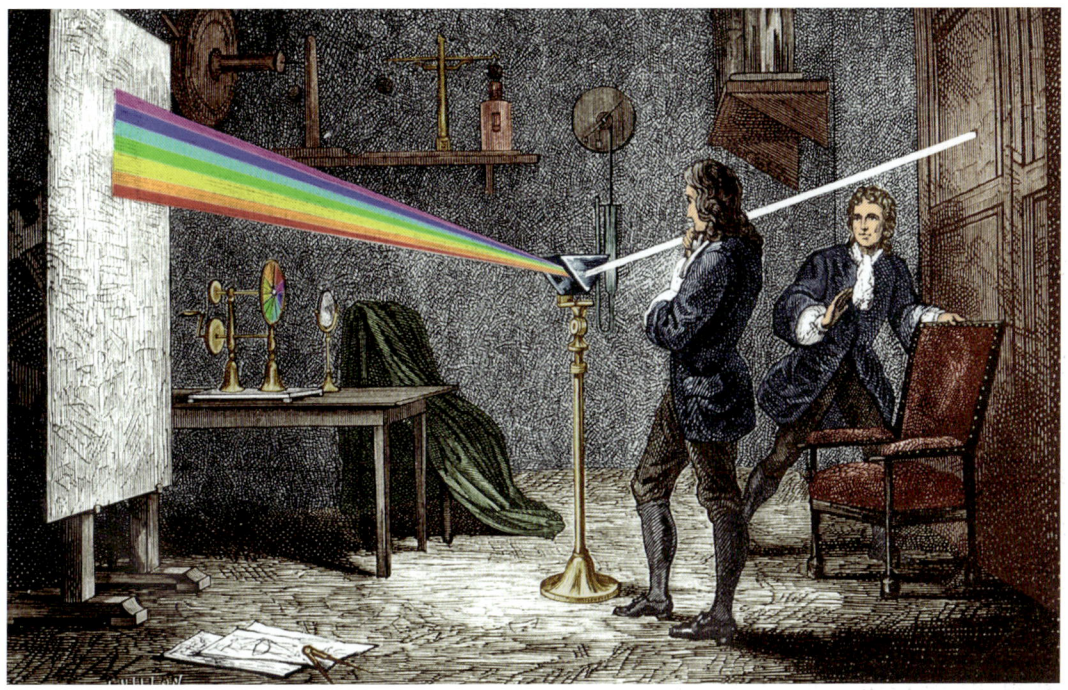

Newton experimented with light and mirrors. He was one of the first to light the "candles" of the Enlightenment.

to found The Royal Society of London for Improving Natural Knowledge. The Royal Society still exists today.

Newton never stopped being fascinated by nature. He spent long childhood hours observing it. His father, a poor and illiterate man, had died before Isaac was born, and his mother was absent for long periods. By all accounts, he was a lonely boy who passed the time inventing mechanical devices and reading. Young Isaac built a tiny windmill that could actually grind corn into cornmeal. He made a clock that used the force of falling water for power.

Isaac had a reputation for being somewhat absentminded—particularly when he settled down with a good book. This reputation was made one day when he got absorbed in his reading and let the sheep he was supposed to be watching run off. (He was fined four shillings, and four pence for his runaway livestock, a considerable sum of money in those days.) Nobody considered young Isaac a genius when he went off to the university, but the world hasn't been the same since.

What Goes Up Must Come Down!

At age nineteen, Newton entered Cambridge, one of England's finest universities, where he studied mathematics. Newton's interests took him outside the college walls, too. He read books before his professors assigned them and learned about chemistry (which wasn't taught at universities in those days) from a local pharmacist.

While Newton was at Cambridge, a deadly disease spread through England. The plague of 1665 shut down many public places, including the university. People fled from cities, hoping to escape the disease. Newton returned to his childhood home in the country. There he waited out the **epidemic** with little to do but think. Those two years at home were the most productive of his life.

There is a well-known story about how Newton made his most famous discovery in one of his solitary moments. Here's how the story goes: Young Isaac Newton was sitting in his garden when *plop!*—an apple fell from a tree and knocked him on the head. What would most people have done about that apple? They might have ignored it or, perhaps, eaten it. But Isaac asked, "What caused the apple to fall down in the first place?" His question led him to discover the theory that a force pulls objects to Earth, a force called **gravity**.

Newton wondered, "Could the same laws of gravity that attract objects to Earth apply to other parts of the universe? Why does the moon stay in its orbit? What keeps it from flying off into space?"

Scholars before Newton had already made important discoveries about our solar system. Do you remember Copernicus and Galileo? In the 1500s,

> ## Vocabulary
>
> **epidemic,** n. a situation in which a disease spreads to many people in an area or region
>
> **gravity,** n. the gravitational force that occurs between Earth and other bodies; the force acting to pull objects toward Earth
>
> **scholar,** n. a person who specializes in a specific academic subject; an expert

No one knows whether the apple story is true, but Newton did formulate the theory of the law of gravity.

Copernicus concluded that Earth moves around the sun. In the early 1600s, Galileo used his telescope to find the evidence that proved Copernicus was right. (But, as you may recall, they both had plenty of trouble getting the Catholic Church to accept the fact that Earth orbits the sun.) It was left to Newton to explain what held the heavenly bodies in place in the sky.

Newton thought of the falling apple. He reasoned that the laws of science that apply on Earth must also apply everywhere else—in other words, he said, these are universal laws of science. The same force of gravity that attracted the apple, he said, keeps the moon in orbit around Earth. It also keeps the planets in orbit around the sun. (But, you might ask, if gravity makes the apple fall to the ground, then why doesn't it make the moon fall to Earth? That's because the moon is moving very fast as it orbits Earth.

The moon orbits Earth at a speed of 2,288 miles per hour.

The speed of the moon, which pushes it outward away from Earth, is exactly balanced by the force of gravity that pulls it toward Earth.)

Questions About the Natural World

As a young man, Newton thought of little but the natural world. His passion for experimenting led him to try some foolish experiments. Once, he stared at the sun with one eye until he could no longer bear it. He wanted to see what would happen. As a result, Newton nearly blinded himself and had to stay shut up in a dark room for several days.

Newton asked many questions about the world around him and the way things work. Through experiments and observation he developed laws of motion. He concluded that a body remains either at rest or in motion in a straight line unless it is affected by some outside force. In other words, if you throw a ball, it will continue to move in a line until something changes its motion. That something could be a baseball bat or a catcher's mitt. It could also be the force of gravity drawing it down to the ground, or wind resistance slowing it down.

Newton had a number of amazing ideas and discoveries in a very short period of time. He finished his first investigation of gravity and the laws of motion when he was only twenty-four. He also invented calculus during that same period. Did he publish his discoveries and immediately change the scientific and mathematical worlds? No, he did not! He was young and uneasy about publishing them. Even after Newton graduated from Cambridge and became a professor there, he put forth his views with caution. Some people accused him of keeping secrets and not wanting to share his findings. Actually, he was a modest man who disliked arguing. He held back because he dreaded criticism. It took great courage for Newton to publish each new idea.

Knowledge Through Reason

After two and a half years of solitary study, Newton produced a major body of writing. His *Philosophiae Naturalis Principia Mathematica,* or *Mathematical Principles,* explained the law of gravity and laws of motion in mathematical terms.

Newton did not publish it immediately—perhaps because he understood the "gravity" of his discoveries. He had just begun to teach at the university. He knew his findings were revolutionary and would likely upset people.

Then, several English scholars approached Newton with a question that he could answer because of his early work. Newton lent these scientists his *Principia,* and they were amazed. They urged Newton to publish this important work, and one of them even offered to pay for the printing. This work was published in 1687.

The publication of the *Principia* is one of the great events in the history of science and thought. Here was the first work to set forth mathematical principles for the operation of the natural world. Newton insisted that certain basic laws of nature held true throughout the whole physical world. These principles, he explained, could be discovered through the use of observation and reason.

Isaac Newton inspired confidence in science and reason. He showed that, through inquiry, or investigation, as well as observation, calculation, and experimentation, it was possible to understand many of nature's laws. People read his work and became more optimistic about human prospects and progress.

Thanks to Newton, more and more people gained confidence in human reason and observation as a way of understanding and explaining the world around them. Thinkers now asked: "If we can use reason to understand the laws of the physical world, can we use reason to understand 'laws' in other areas, too? Can reason help us understand human behavior?" They began to examine politics, religion, and society. To an even greater extent, they observed the world around them and asked questions.

It was Newton who had opened the door to a new understanding of the world, and the people of his era knew it. Alexander Pope, a famous poet of the 1700s, put it this way: "Nature and Nature's laws lay hid in night: God said, 'Let Newton be!', and all was light." This modest man, this intellectual giant, became the first scientist ever knighted by an English queen. Sir Isaac Newton lit a very bright candle in the Age of Reason.

MATHEMATICAL

PRINCIPLES

OF

NATURAL PHILOSOPHY.

By Sir ISAAC NEWTON, Knight.

TRANSLATED INTO ENGLISH, AND ILLUSTRATED WITH A
COMMENTARY,

By ROBERT THORP, M.A.

VOLUME THE FIRST. *no more publ.*
BM

LONDON:
PRINTED FOR W. STRAHAN; AND T. CADELL, IN THE STRAND.
MDCCLXXVII.

74B.

This is an image of the title page of Volume I of Newton's *Principia*. Because the *Principia* was written in Latin, scholars all over Europe could read it easily and be influenced by Newton's work. It was also translated into other languages.

Chapter 2
René Descartes

The Soldier The young soldier sat writing in his tent. He was a frail, well-educated French gentleman. It was not unusual for young gentlemen of the 1600s to become soldiers of fortune—that is, soldiers who joined armies not to fight for a great cause but for travel and adventure.

The Big Question

Why is Descartes considered to be the father of modern philosophy?

This fellow was not writing a letter home or jotting notes about the day's events. He was recording ideas about the workings of the universe and how we know

Vocabulary

philosophy, n. the study of ideas about knowledge, life, and truth; literally, love of wisdom

what we know. The young soldier was René Descartes (/ruh*nay/day*kahrt/). He would become known as the "father of modern **philosophy**." As you read on, you'll get to know this young soldier and learn how he began a revolution in thought.

Descartes (1596–1650) spent much of his life thinking and writing.

Young René

As a boy, René Descartes lived with his grandmother. His mother had died when he was about one year old. René enjoyed being alone in the garden with time to think. Shortly after turning ten, he was sent to boarding school. Because René was often sick as a child, he was allowed to sleep late before taking up his studies for the day.

After boarding school, René went on to study law because that is what his family expected him to do. However, he had no real interest in law. As a young man, René still enjoyed sleeping late and being alone to think, but he also discovered that he loved to travel. This love of travel may be the reason René joined the army. At twenty-two, he went to Holland (today called the Netherlands) and signed on as an unpaid officer in the Dutch army.

Awakening

During his time in Holland, Descartes became fascinated with mathematics and wrote several papers on the subject. He spent just over a year there. Then he traveled for a summer before joining the Bavarian army. (Bavaria was once a kingdom; today it is part of Germany.) A soldier's life is usually pictured as difficult, but in Bavaria, Descartes managed to keep up his old habits of rising late and spending time alone with his thoughts.

He was content with life until the snows came and temperatures quickly dropped below freezing. It was during this time, when Descartes spent long hours

This illustration from the 1800s shows that even as a soldier, Descartes found time to think and to read.

huddled up for warmth and deep in thought, that he had two important insights. He described them as moments of light that showed him great truths about life.

"I Think, Therefore I Am"

Although Descartes was a devout Catholic and always kept a strong belief in God, he also placed high value on human reason. He used reason to explore the human condition and to explain his belief in God. Descartes's use of reason began what we know today as the modern age of philosophy.

After his time in the army, Descartes went back to Holland. For young thinkers, that was the place to explore new ideas and express them freely. Unlike other European nations at the time, Holland did not punish those who questioned religious or political traditions. In the 1600s, Holland, a Protestant country, became the center of the European printing industry. New ideas thrived there like nowhere else in Europe.

Descartes became best known for his book *Discourse on Method.* In its introduction, he takes his reader back to the winter in snow-covered Bavaria. He explains that it was there that he began to doubt and to question. He bases his thinking on the idea that there is only one thing in this world we can be sure of—our thoughts and therefore our own existence. Descartes writes, "There is just one thing that is undeniable: I am thinking. This alone proves my existence." He recognized that whether his thoughts were right or wrong, they were his thoughts. If he was thinking them, he must, in fact, exist. He concludes in Latin: "*Cogito ergo sum.*" In English, this means: "I think, therefore I am." With this certainty about his own existence and his powers of reasoning, Descartes set out to question everything else in the universe. He left this message for other truth-seekers: "It is not enough just to have a fine mind; the main thing is to learn how to apply it properly."

Descartes had promised himself "never to accept anything as true if I did not clearly know it to be so." The notion that the truths of the universe could

DISCOVRS
DE LA METHODE
POVR BIEN CONDVIRE SA RAISON,
ET CHERCHER LA VERITE' DANS LES SCIENCES.
PLVS
LA DIOPTRIQVE
ET LES METEORES,

Qui font des effais de cette METHODE.

PAR RENE' DESCARTES.

Reueuë, & corrigée en cette derniere Edition.

À PARIS,

Chez THEODORE GIRARD, dans la Grand'Salle du Palais,
proche la Porte de la Gallerie Dauphine, du cofté de la
Cour des Aydes, à l'Enuie.

M. DC. LXVIII.
AVEC PRIVILEGE DV ROY.

Descartes's words, "I think, therefore I am," are often quoted. This image shows the title page of his book *Discourse on Method*.

be learned by observation and reason, and not accepted by faith alone, changed the way many people thought. Descartes encouraged people to doubt everything except their own existence until they proved each thing to be true.

The Price of Fame

Descartes became famous throughout Europe. When his work caught the attention of twenty-three-year-old Queen Christina of Sweden, she invited him to her court. The idea of a long trip to chilly Sweden did not excite the fifty-three-year-old philosopher. But the young and intelligent queen got her way.

Each day of Descartes's ill-fated visit began with a brisk sleigh ride over icy streets. He was used to sleeping late and always hated the cold. Within two weeks, he had pneumonia. The great philosopher died in Sweden, having introduced the world to a new way of thinking about what we know and how we know it. Because of his insistence on reason, we remember Descartes as the father of modern philosophy.

Chapter 3
Thomas Hobbes

Long Life A European living in the 1600s had little chance of living past the age of forty. Against all odds, Thomas Hobbes (1588–1679) more than doubled that life expectancy. Born in 1588 in the English village of Malmesbury, Hobbes lived to be ninety-one. It was a long and difficult life.

The Big Question

Why did Thomas Hobbes believe in the need for an all-powerful ruler as the leader of the government?

This was a stormy era for his country's government, and through it all, Hobbes had something to say. Often his ideas were not what people wanted to hear. At times, he was forced to flee for his life and burn his own writings. Thomas Hobbes was certainly not the most popular philosopher of his times. Who was this man? And what did he say that put people in such an uproar?

Thomas Hobbes lived to the age of ninety-one, over twice the average life expectancy for the time.

THOMAS HOBBES Æ Suæ LXXX 1676

Young Thomas Hobbes

Thomas Hobbes entered Oxford University when he was only fifteen years old. By the standards of the time, that was young to be entering college, but not as young as you might think. The typical student began university studies between ages sixteen and eighteen.

After graduation, Hobbes became a tutor for the son of a nobleman. His position included traveling with his pupil, who was only a few years younger than he was. Hobbes would continue his tutoring career for many years. Traveling abroad in Europe with young noblemen gave him the chance to meet interesting people. In France, Hobbes met with Descartes.

Each time Hobbes returned to England, he came back to political unrest. The problem was a conflict between the king and **Parliament**. As you have read, the ruling monarchs in those days, in this case the Stuarts, believed in the divine right of kings. These rulers did not want to grant Parliament any lawmaking powers—the ability to write and pass laws. The struggle between Parliament and the king went on for decades.

> **Vocabulary**
>
> **Parliament,** n. the original lawmaking branch of the English government that is made up of the House of Lords and the House of Commons

Hobbes supported the king in this conflict. When he saw Parliament threatening to take control from the Stuarts, he worried about his own safety. The philosopher fled to France and settled in Paris.

The English Parliament did finally seize control. King Charles I was tried before a court, convicted, and executed. His son, Prince Charles, sought safety in Paris, where Hobbes tutored him in mathematics. They developed a friendship that would one day protect Hobbes.

King Charles I was tried and eventually executed. Thomas Hobbes did not support the removal of the king from the throne.

Hobbes Is Heard

With an eye on the ever-changing and often violent English political scene, Hobbes drew his own conclusions about the purpose and nature of government. In the spirit of the Enlightenment, Hobbes observed events and used his mind to reason about what should be.

Hobbes put forth his ideas in several works. His most famous book, *Leviathan* (/luh*vye*uh*thun/), was published while Hobbes was in France. A leviathan, or sea monster, appears in the Bible as an all-powerful ruler of the seas. In his book, Hobbes argues that government should be all-powerful, like the leviathan.

Hobbes provides reasons why he thought government should be all-powerful. He starts by describing human beings in what he called the "state of nature." Hobbes goes on to say that people are naturally cruel, greedy, and selfish. He explains that they have two main desires: to feel pleasure and to avoid pain. People will do just about anything to meet those selfish ends, Hobbes believed.

A leviathan, or sea monster, is pictured on the title page of Hobbes's book.

Because people were so naturally selfish, Hobbes did not expect that they, when left to their own devices, could be trusted to make choices that would benefit the entire community or even preserve order.

Hobbes was a **pessimist** about human nature, and it was his pessimism that made him believe in strong government. Hobbes looked at the chaos and war of his own century and concluded that, without a strong government, people would live in a constant state of war. In his most famous statement, Hobbes said that without government, human life would be "solitary, poor, nasty, brutish, and short."

What should be done about this unhappy condition? Was there any hope? Hobbes thought a strong government was the answer. He wrote that people must enter into a **"social contract."** As part of this contract, they must give up some of their individual freedoms and turn them over to a powerful leader or assembly. Strong leaders, strict laws, and stiff punishments would protect selfish individuals from waging war on each other. Society would best be served, Hobbes believed, by an **absolute monarchy** with an all-powerful ruler. Only such a government—a leviathan—could ensure peace and safety.

You might ask: What about freedom? Did Hobbes picture a world in which everyone was a slave to government? Hobbes's argument may surprise you

Vocabulary

pessimist, n. a person who tends to see the worst in a situation or who believes the worst will happen

social contract, n. an agreement among individuals in a society and a ruler or government; individuals give up some of their freedoms in exchange for protection by the ruler or government

"absolute monarchy," (phrase) a government in which the king or queen has the unchecked authority to do whatever they want without any restrictions

by its logic and the way that he defines freedom. Hobbes argued that real human freedom is the ability to live peacefully without being threatened by others. Because, in his opinion, people are naturally selfish and cruel, there must be strong laws to protect us from each other. A forceful government, according to Hobbes, does not limit a person's liberty. Quite the opposite: it is the forceful government protecting people from their worst impulses that actually makes real liberty possible.

Pupil Crowned King

When things quieted down in England, Hobbes returned home. In 1660, the monarchy was restored, and his former pupil, Prince Charles, became King Charles II. For several years, Hobbes published his ideas without incident. Then came two terrible years for the English. The plague swept England in 1665, and a great fire destroyed much of London in 1666. People sought comfort in their religious faith, and soon anyone who spoke against religion was in trouble.

Much of London was destroyed in the Great Fire of London. The fire started in a bakery on September 2, 1666.

Many people saw Hobbes and his ideas about the brutish nature of human beings as unchristian. They wanted to ban *Leviathan* and banish the philosopher. Fearful for his safety, Hobbes burned many of his papers. Luckily, his former pupil King Charles II spoke up for the philosopher and protected him. The king did, however, forbid Hobbes from publishing any more of his writings. When Hobbes presented another major work, *Behemoth* (/bih*hee*muth/), the king banned its publication. *Behemoth* was not published until three years after Hobbes's death.

Hobbes's Importance

In his old age, Hobbes was largely ignored by fellow philosophers and scientists. Although he insisted on his own belief in God, most saw him as a threat to religion. He continued to submit papers, but his works were turned away. The elderly Hobbes has been described as an angry, bitter man.

So why was Hobbes important? He put forth a dark view of human nature and a very **authoritarian** model of how society should be organized. People as individuals, he contended, are not basically good. A strong government or a strong leader is necessary to make laws for the peace and safety of the population. Keep his ideas in mind as you read on. And get ready to meet other thinkers whose views differed sharply from those of Thomas Hobbes.

> **Vocabulary**
>
> **authoritarian,** adj. requiring absolute obedience to a ruler or government; not allowing personal freedom

Chapter 4
John Locke

Rights Versus Rulers People have certain **natural rights**. A monarch's right to rule depends on the consent, or agreement, of the people. If a monarch rules poorly, people can and should throw him out.

The Big Question

In what ways did the philosophies of Thomas Hobbes and John Locke differ?

Vocabulary

natural rights, n. rights that all people are born with and that cannot be taken away by the government

These were bold ideas in England in the 1600s. People could get in big trouble for having such thoughts. Yet the Enlightenment spirit and confidence in human reason gave the English philosopher John Locke (1632–1704) the courage to speak his mind. Locke's ideas about government were very different from those of Thomas Hobbes. While Hobbes believed government should be all-powerful, Locke believed the job of government was to protect the natural rights, or liberties, of its subjects. If the government failed to do that, he said, the people should overturn it and create a new government.

The King's Scholar

Young John Locke was a fine student. He was named a "king's scholar" at Westminster School and awarded a scholarship to Oxford University. Locke spent thirty years studying, tutoring, and writing at Oxford.

John Locke had faith in people's ability to learn to live together peacefully.

For thinkers such as John Locke, the late 1600s were good years to be in school. Teachers encouraged students to use reason and to experiment, to think deeply about everything from science and government to religious faith.

Locke studied medicine and became a medical doctor. However, he never earned a living as a doctor. Locke's fame came from his writings about human knowledge and politics. John Locke's ideas launched a new era of thought in England that eventually echoed around the world.

Locke on Knowledge: The Blank Page

What book was top of the best-seller list in the late 1600s? Everyone who was anyone was reading Locke's *Essay Concerning Human Understanding*. In this book, Locke puts forth an important idea about the way human beings think and learn. Each person, he states, comes into this world with a mind like a *tabula rasa*—that's Latin for a blank tablet, like a blank sheet of paper. We have no knowledge at birth, said Locke. Instead, all of our knowledge comes through experience.

Locke explains, "If a child were kept in a place where he never saw any other [colors] but black and white till he were a man, he would have no . . . ideas of scarlet [red] or green."

So how do we get the ideas to fill up our blank page? According to Locke, like Bacon before him, our senses provide us with experience. We learn about our world by seeing, hearing, smelling, tasting, and touching.

John Locke wrote about human nature and how a person's environment impacts their behavior.

We reflect on, or think about, the sensations. We compare them and judge them and then make decisions about our lives.

While Thomas Hobbes described people as being naturally selfish and warlike, Locke took a very different view. He saw human nature as neither good and kind nor bad and violent. He explained that people become what they are because of the events they experience. A person who has known only fighting and cruelty will likely be violent and cruel. In a later book on education, Locke advised parents to treat their children with tenderness and kindness, so that they too would learn to be kind.

Locke on Politics: "Life, Liberty, and Property"

John Locke believed that people, given the right experiences, could be reasonable and moral. He also believed that all people are born with certain natural rights. These, he insisted, include the right to "life, liberty, and property." Locke took a bold stand. It is the government's *duty,* he declared, to preserve the rights of the citizens. What happens if a government denies people their rights or fails to protect those rights? Locke claimed that if a government fails to protect the natural rights of its people, those people have the right to revolt and overthrow the government. It was an idea that would sweep through Europe and across the Atlantic to England's American colonies.

The Mysterious Dr. van der Linden

When King James II sat on the throne of England in the 1680s, he was an unpopular ruler. He set aside Parliament's laws and appointed Catholics to high offices. Many people feared he would disband Parliament and take power away from the Protestant Church of England.

King James was not a fan of John Locke. He was well aware of Locke's political views. Unlike Hobbes, who had favored an absolute monarchy, Locke had sided with Parliament in its struggle against the Stuarts. Now there were rumors that Locke supported a plot to overthrow the king. The philosopher's name soon appeared on a list of persons wanted for **treason**.

Fearing for his life, Locke fled to Holland, where he went into hiding under the name Dr. van der Linden. Locke was not about to be silenced by threats. He wrote that he would continue to love truth and to seek it without worrying about "whom it pleases or displeases." He used his time in Holland to complete his *Essay Concerning Human Understanding*.

While in Holland, Locke met Prince William of Orange, husband of James II's daughter, Mary. Locke became one of Prince William's supporters. In 1688, Parliament unseated King James II and invited William and Mary to come from Holland to take the English throne. Locke returned to England as a companion to Mary. For Locke, it was more than a chance to return home in safety. John Locke was a philosopher who got to see his ideas put to use.

King James II did not agree with John Locke's political views and believed that they challenged the monarchy.

Parliament attached conditions to its invitation to William and Mary. To become king and queen, William and Mary had to give up many of their royal powers to Parliament, limiting the strength of the monarchy. Parliament also called for a **bill of rights**.

This change in government in 1688 was called the Glorious Revolution. Unlike most revolutions, there was no bloodshed or violence, but it was one of the most important changes in government in history. From 1688 onward, no

William and Mary are shown here with all the symbols—crowns, scepters, and the royal coat of arms—of English monarchs.

king or queen could rule in England without the consent of Parliament. England had taken a giant step on the path to liberty.

Locke's **radical** ideas had become a reality. The English people had overthrown one ruler and replaced him with another ruler who respected their natural rights. It would not be the last time that this would happen in history. Enlightenment ideas were taking shape elsewhere as well. In Scotland, for instance, with thinkers such as David Hume and Adam Smith. They were also having an impact on life across the English Channel in France.

Chapter 5
The Enlightenment in France

Speech and Freedom In France in the 1700s, most writers chose their words carefully. Freedom of speech was not a guarantee. The wrong comment written or spoken about the monarch or his court could put a French citizen in the Bastille (/ba*stee*yuh/), a prison for those who dared to displease their government.

The Big Question

Why did Montesquieu believe that it was important to limit the power of a ruler and of any one branch of government?

The Bastille was both a fortress and a prison in Paris, France.

But threats of prison did not silence the voices of the Enlightenment. In earlier years, scientists and philosophers, such as Newton, Descartes, Hobbes, and Locke, had opened eyes and minds. Like them, thinkers of the 1700s had powerful ideas. They would find a way to be heard.

The Baron

Charles-Louis de Secondat was born a noble and had a grand title, Baron de Montesquieu (/mohn*tes*kyoo/). He inherited wealth and a government position. He did not, however, spend his life idly enjoying high society. Instead, Baron de Montesquieu became one of the most important authors of the 1700s.

When it came to politics, the baron knew what he was talking about. He had traveled around Europe and watched government at work in Italy and England. He'd read widely about ancient and medieval times and about Chinese and Native American cultures.

In the spirit of the Enlightenment, Montesquieu observed, studied, and reasoned. Then he drew this conclusion: France was in big trouble. Montesquieu saw most of the people suffering poverty and injustice. A strict **social order** enforced by the monarch and **clergy** allowed no chance for change.

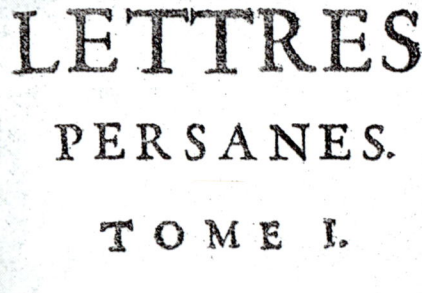

Baron de Montesquieu (1689–1755) was the real author of *The Persian Letters*.

Yes, Montesquieu was a wise man. He was wise enough to know that if he openly criticized the French government or the Church, he could be imprisoned. So he wrote in secret. Like others you've read about, Montesquieu did much of his work in Holland. In 1721, he published *The Persian Letters*. As far as readers knew, the authors were Usbek and Rica, two travelers from Persia who were exploring France. The book was a collection of their letters home. The clever, humorous Persians were pure fiction, but readers recognized their criticisms of the French ruling class as absolutely true to real life.

On the King and His Court

In one of his first letters home, Usbek explains that he and Rica had left their quiet lives to search for wisdom. "Our purpose," Usbek writes, "is to educate ourselves about the customs and social arrangements in the West."

Remember, as fictional characters, Usbek and Rica had nothing to fear from the French government. They could speak freely, whereas Montesquieu could not.

The book, *The Persian Letters,* was a hit. Readers laughed out loud. They also recognized some harsh truths, such as when Rica reports on the king of France. Why, the clever monarch could make people who had always used coins to buy and sell goods believe that paper was money! "This king is a great magician," Rica declares, explaining that when the monarch ran low on money to support his wars, all he had to do was have some printed.

Baron de Montesquieu found a clever way to spread his ideas.

Presto! More money! If making money were that simple, everyone would be rich.

In another letter, Usbek speaks his mind about the French court. He describes the life of a court nobleman trying to "conceal the fact that he has nothing to do by looking busy."

Montesquieu's Pen Strikes Again

It did not take long for fans to figure out that the real author of *The Persian Letters* was none other than the Baron de Montesquieu. He soon published again, this time using his own name. In *The Spirit of the Laws,* Montesquieu bases his writings on what he'd learned about the governments of the world. He praises the British for limiting the power of the monarch and protecting the rights of the people.

Vocabulary

separation of powers, n. the division of responsibilities among multiple branches of government

What is the best way to protect liberty? In *The Spirit of the Laws,* Montesquieu puts forward an important idea. He suggests that a country must limit the power of its ruler and, in fact, of any one branch of government. This could best be done, he explains, with a "**separation of powers**."

Montesquieu pictured a government in which the monarch held the executive power, a parliament made the laws, and courts enforced justice. He believed that each branch of government could check the power of the other two. Montesquieu's thoughts on checks and balances would

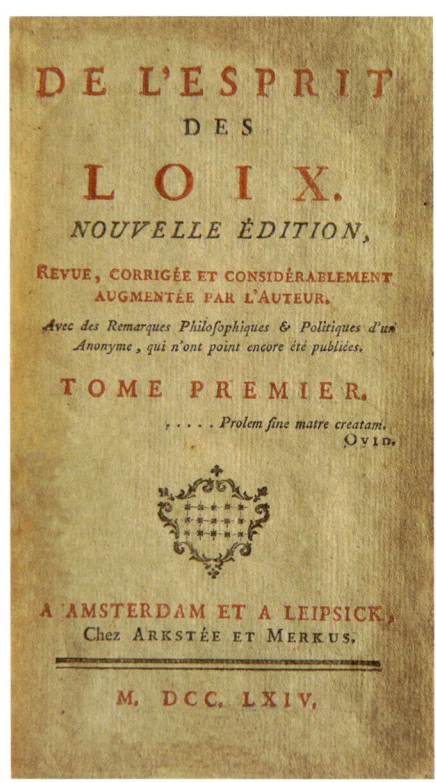

As a nobleman, Montesquieu could have lived a life of ease, unconcerned about people less fortunate than he was. However, he chose to work on innovative ideas about ways to improve how society functioned.

one day become part of the U.S. Constitution. You will read more about this in the next chapter.

At about the same time that Montesquieu suggested dividing government powers, he also fiercely attacked slavery. He wrote that enslaving a person because of color was not a reasonable act. It was no more logical than enslaving someone because of "a long or short face." In *The Spirit of the Laws,* Montesquieu describes slavery as "the most shocking violation of nature."

The baron did not suggest extreme social changes. He did not call for rebellion or democracy. Rather he sought peaceful, modest reforms that would give people happier lives. He pictured a wise, enlightened monarch who listened to the people and whose power was held in check by a parliament and courts of justice.

The Prisoner

Now let's go behind the walls of the Bastille. Once a military fortress protecting the city of Paris, the Bastille had become a royal prison. It is just four years before Montesquieu published *The Persian Letters.* A young man, François Marie Arouet (/ah*roo*ay/), is locked in the Bastille. What is his

> **Vocabulary**
>
> **pseudonym,** n.
> a fake name,
> frequently used
> by authors

crime? He has written verses making fun of the French government! For eleven months, the young author continues his writing behind the stone walls of the Bastille. Now he uses the **pseudonym** Voltaire (/vohl*tair/). It would become an extremely famous pen name!

Like other Enlightenment thinkers, Voltaire examined society and then launched a battle to improve it. His weapon was his wit. Voltaire targeted greedy officials, lazy nobles, and evil institutions. He hated slavery and religious intolerance. Voltaire used humor to point out social wrongs and to demand change. His remarks made the ruling classes seem foolish. The French government had largely ignored Montesquieu's criticisms, accepting

After Voltaire (1694–1778) was freed, he traveled to England.

them as simple teasing. After all, Montesquieu was one of them—a noble himself. But Voltaire was a commoner, an ordinary man. His comments could not be allowed!

Voltaire was released, but he was not out of the Bastille for long before his sharp wit landed him in trouble again. This time he insulted a powerful young nobleman. (Some say he challenged the fellow to a duel.) The incident left Voltaire with two choices: he could go back to jail, or he could flee to England.

Voltaire took the reasonable choice and lived in England for three years. As he most likely studied the philosophy of John Locke and the science of Isaac Newton, he became more certain than ever that his homeland faced serious problems. He felt that England, with its **limited monarchy**, had the answers.

In a letter home to a friend, Voltaire wrote, "In this country [England] it is possible to use one's mind freely and nobly, without fear or cringing."

Voltaire had strong feelings about freedom of expression. "My trade," he said, "is to say what I think." He refused to be silenced. As soon as Voltaire returned to Paris, he published again. In a book called *Letters on the English,* he made heroes of Bacon, Locke, and Newton and praised their country for its science and philosophy. It was a country, he said, that protected the rights of its people.

Daring publishers secretly printed Voltaire's newest works. When copies appeared in Paris, the order went out: "Arrest Voltaire! Burn his books!" But the book burnings backfired. As soon as his books were forbidden, more people wanted to read them.

Thoughts from Ferney

Voltaire was not interested in spending any more time behind the walls of the Bastille. He again fled Paris. He bought an estate at Ferney, near the border of France and Switzerland. There he lived out his life, but not in silence.

Voltaire continued to write books, plays, pamphlets, and letters. From his country estate came the sharp-tongued voice of reason that spoke out against **censorship**, ignorance, and injustice.

> ### Vocabulary
>
> **"limited monarchy,"** (phrase) a government in which the power of the king or queen is restricted by a governing body such as Parliament
>
> **censorship,** n. the practice of removing or prohibiting books, art, films, or other media that the government finds offensive, immoral, or harmful

A steady stream of visitors kept Voltaire from being lonely at Ferney. In fact, his many guests nicknamed him "the innkeeper of Europe." There must have been some lively discussions at Ferney. Voltaire never failed to stand up against oppression and injustice. An argument with a visitor may have prompted him to declare this famous line: "I do not agree with a word that you say, but I will defend to the death your right to say it!"

Voices of Change

Voltaire and Montesquieu set examples for other free thinkers to follow. In the coffeehouses and parlors of Paris, people were meeting and talking. Some met in small private groups known as salons. They were usually hosted by women. The French thinkers became known as *philosophes,* (/fee*law*zawfs/), which means lovers of wisdom. The *philosophes* discussed and debated ways to achieve a fairer society. They expressed their ideas in books and pamphlets. Voltaire was among the group of *philosophes* who wrote and published the great *Encyclopédie* (*Encyclopedia* in English). In more than thirty large volumes that were published over twenty years, they summed up the major ideas and discoveries of the Enlightenment.

At first these new ideas about freedom, rights and liberty, and calls for reform remained within the upper and middle classes. Despite the efforts of Montesquieu and Voltaire, and others, including the brilliant Jean Jacques Rousseau (/zhahn/ zhack/roo*soh/), the Enlightenment had not yet reached the masses of people.

Enlightenment Reaches the People

Not until the late 1700s did the message of the Enlightenment begin to reach the ordinary people of Paris. It seeped from the city into rural villages, where peasants still toiled each day and paid high taxes—just as they always had.

At last, the masses began to question the way things were. They began to see the possibility of a better life in a fairer world. They imagined a society that protected rights—one in which people could speak their minds. Europe's once-powerful royals had failed. The message was out, and there was no turning back.

ELÉMENS

DE LA

PHILOSOPHIE

DE NEUTON,

Mis à la portée de tout le monde.

Par Mʀ. DE VOLTAIRE.

A AMSTERDAM,

Chez JACQUES DESBORDES.

M. DCC. XXXVIII.

In 1738, Voltaire published the *Elements of the Philosophy of Newton*, bringing Newton's theories to France.

Chapter 6
The Enlightenment in Action

Ideas Across the Ocean "I hold that a little rebellion now and then is a good thing, and as necessary in the political world as storms in the physical."
—Thomas Jefferson

The Big Question

In what ways did Europe's Enlightenment thinkers inspire America's Founding Fathers to create a government by the people, for the people?

Although these words were not actually about rebelling against the British, Thomas Jefferson was making it clear that rebellion is at times inevitable. When American colonists became unhappy under the heavy hand of Great Britain's rule, they defended their liberty and launched a revolution. The fact is that many of the revolutionaries' ideas—and some of the words they used to declare independence—echoed Britain's and France's greatest thinkers. The spirit of the Enlightenment had crossed the Atlantic Ocean.

Thomas Jefferson (1743–1826) believed that the government of a nation has a duty to provide and protect the best interests of the people it serves.

What should citizens do if their government takes away their liberty? According to the Enlightenment thinker John Locke, it is the duty of those citizens to protest. They must demand change. What if the government does not listen to their demands? Then they must replace that government with a new one.

Thomas Jefferson: An Enlightened Man

In 1776, American colonists decided they could no longer **tolerate** Great Britain's rule. They were tired of paying taxes while having no voice in government. The colonists had asked for change. They had demonstrated and protested without the desired results. Finally, they took extreme action. The colonists proclaimed their freedom from Great Britain in the Declaration of Independence.

Do you remember who wrote that famous declaration? A committee of patriots had selected thirty-three-year-old Thomas Jefferson to draft the colonists' formal demands for freedom. "I will do as well as I can," Jefferson promised the committee. He wrote a moving attack against **tyranny** and a call for freedom that people still quote today.

Jefferson was well suited for the task. With private tutors as a child, a college degree, and training in the law, he had had the best education available. He'd made the most of his schooling—reading and studying for long hours each day.

Jefferson seems to have been interested in everything. He examined fossil bones and Native American mounds. He collected books for his library. He observed life and figured out how to make it better. Jefferson invented the first storm windows and a clock that could tell the day of the week as well as the hour. He was a truly enlightened thinker and doer. It is not by chance

Thomas Jefferson was not only a great thinker, he was also an inventor and a builder. The image above shows his desk in the home he built called Monticello, in Virginia. On the desk is a machine he invented that could duplicate, or make copies of, his correspondence.

Thomas Jefferson wrote the Declaration of Independence, but he had some help from Benjamin Franklin (left) and John Adams (middle).

that many parts of the Declaration of Independence echo the ideas of the European Enlightenment. On the walls of his library, Jefferson hung portraits of Bacon, Locke, and Newton, who, he said, were "the three greatest men that have ever lived."

Jefferson began the Declaration of Independence by stating that "all men" are entitled to certain natural rights, including "Life, Liberty, and the pursuit of Happiness." Now, where have you read that before? Like Jefferson, you have studied the ideas of the English philosopher John Locke. In the 1600s, Locke expressed his belief that people are born with natural rights to "life, liberty, and property." In the 1700s, Jefferson's version of the idea suited America, a new world where even people of limited means—those with little property—have a right to seek happiness.

Here's another idea Locke and Jefferson shared. In the late 1600s, Locke declared that a government has a duty to preserve its citizens' natural rights. If their rights are not protected, citizens should change or replace the government. Compare Locke's opinion with this passage from the Declaration of Independence:

> . . . to secure these rights [life, liberty, and the pursuit of happiness], governments are **instituted** among Men, **deriving** their just powers from the consent of the governed. That whenever any Form of Government becomes destructive to these ends, it is the Right of the People to alter or to abolish it, and to institute new Government. . . .

Both Locke and Jefferson described a government that gets its power from the people. That bold, defiant idea—the idea, as Jefferson said, that "governments . . . deriv[e] their just powers from the consent of the governed"—led to the Glorious Revolution of 1688 and the American Revolution that began in 1776. Thomas Jefferson clearly admired the Enlightenment ideas of John Locke and found inspiration in his writings.

Benjamin Franklin: The American *Philosophe*

When you read about Voltaire, you learned that the French word *philosophe* means a lover of wisdom. Benjamin Franklin (1706–1790) became known as an American *philosophe*. Franklin, who lived into his eighties, spent much of his long life seeking knowledge. He read widely. He studied, experimented, invented, and traveled. When Franklin traveled to Britain, he particularly enjoyed his time in Edinburgh. There, he visited with David Hume and other Scottish Enlightenment figures whose works he had read and absorbed. From Philadelphia, Franklin exchanged letters with European thinkers and scientists, including some of the *philosophes* who worked on the French *Encyclopédie*.

Franklin did more than study what others had to offer. He added to the world's store of knowledge himself. He was a witty author who wrote these gems of wisdom: "Three may keep a secret, if two of them are dead." Or "Fish and visitors smell after three days." Franklin included such memorable sayings in his *Poor Richard's Almanack*. Like other annual almanacs, Franklin's was based on a calendar, but his was more entertaining and contained more useful information. He aimed to help people improve themselves. Franklin also helped Jefferson write the Declaration of Independence.

As a scientist, the enlightened Franklin experimented with electricity and invented the lightning rod. He also invented bifocal glasses. He encouraged others to invent things too.

This image shows Benjamin Franklin demonstrating to his son that lightning is electricity.

Franklin helped to found the American Philosophical Society as a place for discussion. Like the Royal Society in England, the American Philosophical Society still exists today. As a politician and **diplomat**, he traveled to France, seeking support for America's revolution against Great Britain. Franklin was a hit in Paris. He was a welcome addition to intellectual discussions.

An Enlightened Government

You may have learned how the **delegates** to America's Constitutional Convention wrote a code of laws for the new independent nation. Among these delegates was James Madison of Virginia, whose work at the convention earned him the nickname "Father of the Constitution." Like the European thinkers of the Enlightenment, Madison studied and observed. When faced with the job of drafting a constitution, he threw himself into the task with true Enlightenment spirit.

Picture a hot night in 1787. Although it's nearly midnight, James Madison is awake. In an upstairs chamber of a Philadelphia boarding house, he spends long hours reading and taking notes by candlelight. He lists problems that must be solved. He studies governments of other times and other lands and considers their solutions.

James Madison (1751–1836)

The delegates at the Constitutional Convention signed a document that continues to enlighten the lives of many people, not only in the U.S. but around the world as well.

James Madison, like Jefferson, studied and admired the works of John Locke. He enthusiastically agreed with the notion that officials can only govern with the consent of the people.

James Madison came to each session of the Constitutional Convention inspired by the writings of Europe's Enlightenment thinkers, especially Hume and Montesquieu. The delegates created a document that, according to its own words, aimed to "promote the general welfare." To this day, the U.S. Constitution defines the government of the American people. It is one of the American Enlightenment's most significant productions.

Merci, Monsieur Montesquieu

Merci is the French word for thank you. The young United States definitely owed a thank you to Baron de Montesquieu for his ideas on government.

Remember, Montesquieu had suggested that to protect individual freedoms, a country must limit the power of its ruler. In fact, every branch of government must answer to the other branches. The power of the executive, be it a president or a king, must be balanced by the lawmakers of the legislative branch and the courts of the judicial branch.

If you look at the U.S. Constitution, you should recognize some of Montesquieu's ideas in action. A system of checks and balances keeps any one person or any one branch of government from gaining too much power. The Constitution also uses Montesquieu's ideas of a balanced government by dividing powers between the national government and the states.

Action!

In 1789, the U.S. Constitution became the law of the land. It outlined a government that gave more power to its people than any other government in the world. You have learned that these were not purely American ideas. The European Enlightenment had encouraged dreams of a freer society and a government based on reason. It had sparked the idea of a government created by the people for the purpose of serving the people. The Constitution of the new United States put those ideas into action.

There were more changes to come! The Enlightenment ideals that inspired the American colonists also sparked action in Europe. People in France were ready to demand the personal liberties their great thinkers had been suggesting. They'd heard the ideas of Voltaire and Montesquieu and had watched ideas become reality in America. The *Encyclopédie* had spread the message throughout Europe, across the Atlantic Ocean, and back again. The call for freedom was about to move out of France's coffeehouses and bookstores and onto the streets and battlefields. The French Revolution was about to begin.

The French Revolution was a violent revolt against the royal family and the nobility who had failed to listen to the needs of the people of France. The French king and queen were removed from power and executed.

Glossary

A

"absolute monarchy," (phrase) a government in which the king or queen has the unchecked authority to do whatever they want without any restrictions (25)

authoritarian, adj. requiring absolute obedience to a ruler or government; not allowing personal freedom (27)

B

bill of rights, n. a series of laws that protect the liberties and freedoms of citizens (32)

C

calculus, n. a type of advanced mathematics focused on the study of change (6)

censorship, n. the practice of removing or prohibiting books, art, films, or other media that the government finds offensive, immoral, or harmful (41)

clergy, n. in the Christian Church, people, such as priests, who carry out religious duties (36)

D

delegate, n. a representative (50)

derive, v. to get something from a source (48)

diplomat, n. a person who represents a government in its relationships with other governments (50)

"divine right of kings," (phrase) the belief that kings and queens have a God-given right to rule, and that rebellion against them is a sin (4)

E

epidemic, n. a situation in which a disease spreads to many people in an area or region (8)

G

gravitation, n. the attractive force existing between any two objects that have mass; the force that pulls objects together (6)

gravity, n. the gravitational force that occurs between Earth and other bodies; the force acting to pull objects toward Earth (8)

I

institute, v. to establish or start something new (48)

L

"limited monarchy," (phrase) a government in which the power of the king or queen is restricted by a governing body such as Parliament (41)

N

natural rights, n. rights that all people are born with and that cannot be taken away by the government (28)

P

Parliament, n. the original lawmaking branch of the English government that is made up of the House of Lords and the House of Commons (22)

pessimist, n. a person who tends to see the worst in a situation or who believes the worst will happen (25)

philosophy, n. the study of ideas about knowledge, life, and truth; literally, love of wisdom (14)

pseudonym, n. a fake name, frequently used by authors (39)

R

radical, adj. favoring large or widespread changes (33)

reason, n. the ability of the mind to think clearly and understand; logic (2)

S

scholar, n. a person who specializes in a specific academic subject; an expert (8)

separation of powers, n. the division of responsibilities among multiple branches of government (38)

social contract, n. an agreement among individuals in a society and a ruler or government; individuals give up some of their freedoms in exchange for protection by the ruler or government (25)

social order, n. a system—formed by institutions, organizations, customs, and beliefs—that helps to maintain accepted ways of behaving (36)

T

tolerate, v. to accept different beliefs or practices (46)

treason, n. disloyalty to a country by helping an enemy (32)

tyranny, n. a type of government in which one person illegally seizes all power, usually ruling in a harsh and brutal way; a dictatorship (46)

The French Revolution and Romanticism

Table of Contents

Reader
Core Knowledge History and Geography™

Chapter 1
Roots of the Revolution

The Spread of Ideas In the late 1700s, Paris, France, buzzed with new ideas. People came together to discuss these ideas at social gatherings known as salons. These salons usually took place in the fashionable mansions of the wealthy aristocrats.

The Big Question

Which Enlightenment ideas spread across France, and why might some have considered those ideas to be dangerous?

Baron de Montesquieu

Jean-Jacques Rousseau

Voltaire

Enlightenment thinking spread in the sparkling, elegant atmosphere of the salons, such as the one depicted here, where *philosophes* and aristocrats freely discussed ideas.

The salons attracted writers, poets, musicians, important government officials, and other liberal-minded aristocrats, as well as many members of the rapidly growing middle class.

These people talked about the Enlightenment ideas that were sweeping across Europe: ideas about natural rights, the rights of man, religious tolerance, freedom of speech and of the press, and political freedom to choose their own leaders. For some, ideas about political freedom were considered dangerous as France had a monarchy. The king ruled because he was born to do that very thing.

If you had been a guest at one of these salons, you might have heard about the ideas of John Locke. Locke was an English philosopher who argued that all

people have certain natural rights and that the people of a nation have the right to get rid of any government that takes away these rights. Or you might have heard people refer to one of the French *philosophes* (/fee*luh*zohfs/). The *philosophes* were the thinkers of the Enlightenment. They believed in justice, tolerance, and freedom. They wanted to limit the power of the **absolute monarch** and give the people a voice in government. The most famous *philosophes* were Montesquieu (/mon*tuh*skyooh/), Jean-Jacques Rousseau (/zhahn/zhack/rooh*soh/), and Voltaire (/vohl*tair/).

Aristocratic women, such as Madame Geoffrin seen here in this painting, were an essential part of the salon culture. They promoted Enlightenment ideas.

60

Montesquieu wrote critically of French government and society in the *Persian Letters*. In *The Spirit of the Laws*, he set forth his views, or political theories, on how best to govern. He praised the English for establishing and preserving a balance of power between Parliament and the king. He felt that such balanced government was better than the absolute monarchy of the Bourbon (/boor*buhn/) kings. Bourbon was the family name of the line of kings who had ruled France for two hundred years.

Rousseau was the most radical, or extreme. He complained that people are born free but usually end up enslaved. He summarized the political state of the world in a famous line: "Man is born free and everywhere he is in chains." Rousseau wanted to see those chains broken and destroyed. He also angered the French rulers by insisting that kings should rule by the will of the people, not by the will of God.

Voltaire was the wittiest and most popular of the *philosophes*. He was a great advocate of religious freedom, and he used humor and satire to make his points. He made the French people laugh at his jokes and insults toward the institution he most hated, the Catholic Church. He claimed that the Church deliberately kept people in ignorance and superstition and refused to tolerate any disagreements.

Talk of Change

In the salons of Paris, people could discuss the ideas of these thinkers openly and freely. But elsewhere, they had to be more careful. They were not free to criticize the state (the French government) in public.

Both writings and speech were **censored**. Works of Voltaire and the other *philosophes* had to be circulated in manuscript form or sent to other countries to be printed as books and then smuggled back into France.

> **Vocabulary**
>
> **censor**, v. to remove or prohibit books, art, films, or other media that the government finds offensive, immoral, or harmful

Despite this censorship, Enlightenment ideas continued to spread in France. Many well-educated members of the middle and upper classes found these ideas appealing. They liked the idea of having a voice in government, something they had never had under the rule of the Bourbon kings. Even some members of the aristocracy were growing tired of the king's absolutist ideas and hoped for change. Some of the officials who were supposed to censor books secretly helped banned authors circulate their writings.

Title page of Voltaire's *Elements of the Philosophy of Newton*

By the late 1780s, the ideas of the Enlightenment had been simmering in the minds of French people for decades. Some *philosophes*, including Voltaire, believed that the best road to change was to convince the king to make **reforms**.

> **Vocabulary**
>
> **reform,** n. an improvement

Radical thinkers thought that more drastic steps were needed. They didn't want to rely on the king's goodwill to give them the freedoms they deserved. They wanted to limit the king's power. After all, the English had done it. The French could do it, too.

The Influence of English Rights

Many French thinkers had visited England and been impressed with English freedom. When Voltaire visited in 1726, the English way of government was firmly established. Parliament had passed the Bill of Rights, which forced the king to share power with it and limited the government's right to treat people unfairly, without restrictions. But it had taken a bloody civil war in the 1640s and the Glorious Revolution of 1688–1689 to establish England's limited monarchy.

High officials of the French government worried. In 1649, the English had executed their king, Charles I. Imagine—ordinary people just across the English Channel executing a monarch who ruled by the **divine right of kings**.

The Parliament of England successfully limited the power of kings. Charles I is shown in the painting attempting to rule over the English Parliament, but he was ultimately defeated.

Indeed, English ideas traveled easily to France. Many liberal thinkers, including Voltaire and Montesquieu, believed that the English system was better than their own.

Some French intellectuals began to ask, "Why not France? Why not have a limited monarchy like the English? Why must we continue to suffer the injustices of a **tyrannical** Church and state?"

Enlightenment and America

Meanwhile, the light of these new ideas reached across the ocean to America. Men who would soon risk their lives and fortunes in a revolution against Great Britain enthusiastically absorbed Enlightenment ideas. Americans, such as Benjamin Franklin, James Madison, and Thomas Jefferson, were already well acquainted with the rights won by the English in the Glorious Revolution. They expected those same rights for the American colonists.

Enlightenment ideas gave the American revolutionaries the ammunition they needed to fight for their independence and for a new kind of government, one that went far beyond what many French intellectuals of the time could

Benjamin Franklin   James Madison   Thomas Jefferson

imagine. Soon the French, who had sent their ideas, would send more important help to the American revolutionaries.

Let Me Volunteer

The aristocrat Marquis de Lafayette (/mahr*key/duh/lah*fee*et) believed in the ideals of the Enlightenment, and he wanted to help America's struggle for freedom. Eager to win military fame and glory, he bought his own ship and volunteered to fight with the colonists.

Lafayette risked his life, leading American troops in battle against the British. He showed that he was truly committed to the cause of liberty. Lafayette became a hero of the American Revolution and a hero to his own people in France. He was the first Frenchman to join the American fight, but many others followed him.

Marquis de Lafayette played an important role in the American Revolution and in the French Revolution. He was a fellow soldier and friend of George Washington.

France to the Rescue

The French king, Louis XVI, was an absolute monarch. He had no sympathy for the ideals of the American Revolution. France and Great Britain had been enemies for centuries. The French and Indian War had cost the French enormous sums of money and the loss of almost all of France's territory in North America. Nothing made King Louis happier than seeing the British humiliated by the upstart American revolutionaries, even though he didn't share their beliefs.

In February 1778, France and the United States signed the Treaty of Alliance, agreeing to help each other fight Great Britain. France sent money, equipment, twelve thousand soldiers, thirty-two thousand sailors, and a large naval fleet.

Many of the Frenchmen who fought side by side with the Americans—especially Lafayette—admired the courage of the Americans. They saw firsthand how a handful of determined revolutionaries who believed in the ideals of the Enlightenment could defy a mighty empire. Among the liberal intellectuals in France, the success of the United States made the desire for liberty burn more brightly.

The American Revolution to some extent contributed in an

King Louis XVI of France agreed to help the Americans fight the British.

unexpected way to the French desire for reform. The war was costly. The French **treasury** was still feeling the effects of the very expensive French and Indian War. This, alongside many other problems in France in the 1700s—such as wide-scale dissatisfaction with high taxation, food shortages, economic hardships, and a social structure that gave ordinary people very few rights—would all contribute to a chain of events, the outcome of which was a second major revolution.

Vocabulary

treasury, n. a place where money and other riches of a government are kept

Chapter 2
The Three Estates

Wretched Individuals "Of twenty millions of people supposed to be in France, I am of opinion there are nineteen millions more wretched, more accursed, in every circumstance of human existence, than the most conspicuously wretched individual of the whole United States."

The Big Question

What was life like for the people who belonged to the Third Estate compared to those who made up the First and Second Estates?

Life for French peasants had not changed much since the Middle Ages.

So said Thomas Jefferson, who spent four years in France. Jefferson exaggerated. The "most conspicuously wretched" people in the United States were African American enslaved workers, whose lives were far worse than those of French peasants.

Nevertheless, many French peasants were poor and—if their crops failed, as they often did—hungry. They occupied the bottom rung of a rigid social ladder, the *ancien régime* (/ahnn*syann/ ray*zheem/), or "old **regime**," which had been in place for hundreds of years.

Three Social Classes

Medieval society had been divided into three classes: the clergy, the nobility, and the peasants. By the 1700s, many things had changed, but France was still divided into the same three classes, called the Three Estates.

The First Estate—the clergy—remained much the same. However, the gap between wealthy churchmen and poor churchmen had grown even wider. Most **parish priests** remained poor, while other Church leaders were much richer and more powerful. As the official church in France, the Catholic Church had great power. Wealthy, high-ranking members of the French Catholic Church lived like princes in extravagantly furnished palaces. They often preferred to spend their time at the royal court rather than performing their religious duties.

The clergy's wealth came from **tithes** (/tythz/) and from rents on the land they owned. In fact, in the 1700s, the clergy made up less than 1 percent of the population but owned 10 percent of the land. Although the clergy paid no taxes, they gave about 2 percent of their income as a "gift" to the state. Their wealth and large landholdings meant they had power in guiding the affairs of the nation.

The Second Estate—the nobility or aristocracy—had changed a good deal more than the First Estate. For one thing, it was no longer a warrior class. Although most army officers were nobles, or members of the aristocracy, France no longer needed armored knights to battle invaders.

Overall, nobles owned 20 percent of the land. Some were not particularly well off, and most had only modest wealth, but a few were extremely rich. These few hired managers to look after their property while they lived luxuriously in Paris or at the royal court at Versailles (/ver*sigh/). Nobles had many exclusive privileges. For instance, they often didn't pay taxes, except perhaps in wartime. Aristocrats were the only people allowed to hold the highest offices of the Church, the government, and the military. By the late 1700s, many aristocrats were willing to give up some of these privileges—if the king granted them more political power.

The First and Second Estates had a common interest: holding onto their wealth and power. That meant keeping things pretty much the way they were, unless, of course, they could weaken the king and get a little more power for themselves.

Of all the groups, the **Third Estate** had changed the most since **feudal** times. It also had the best reason to want more change. Everybody who did not belong to the First Estate or the Second Estate belonged to the Third Estate. That included about 98 percent of the population! In feudal times, the Third Estate had been mostly peasants. But by the 1700s, a large middle class had developed within this third branch of the French social structure. There were still millions of peasants, but there were also doctors, lawyers, business people, merchants, manufacturers, writers, government workers, and craftspeople. Anyone who was not a clergyman or an aristocrat fell into this category.

Vocabulary

Third Estate, n. in France, everyone who was not a member of the nobility or clergy; included everyone from the poorest of the poor to the wealthy middle class

feudal, adj. relating to the medieval system of exchanging land for service and loyalty

In France in the 1700s, everyone belonged to one of the three social classes, called Estates. This cartoon shows the burden imposed on many of the people who belonged to the Third Estate by members of the nobility and the clergy.

Classes Within the Third Estate

All of the groups within the Third Estate had reason to be unhappy with the structure of French society. They had spent nearly all of the 1700s under the rule of an absolute monarch. Many felt it was time for a change.

The wealthiest group in the Third Estate was the **bourgeois** (/boorzh*wah/). Some were as rich as nobles, and they dressed like nobles, in powdered wigs, silk stockings, and tight-fitting knee breeches called culottes (/coo*lots/). They were members of the middle class. But no matter how rich they were or how well they dressed, the bourgeois were not of noble birth. A few of the very wealthiest could purchase noble status. The rest were looked down upon by the nobility. Most had to pay taxes (though some bought exemptions). No matter how smart they were or how hard they worked, they could never be promoted to the highest ranks in the Church or in the army.

By the 1700s, the bourgeois had developed a deep resentment against the nobility. After all, the bourgeois argued, they were the ones who supplied most of the money, engaged in trade, and generally did the work of building the wealth of the country. Many nobles did little but sit at court, collect their rents, and waste time and money in silly games. And yet these idle, useless aristocrats had the nerve to look down on the middle class!

The urban working classes within the Third Estate were nearly as poor as the peasants. They were the stonemasons, furniture makers, butchers, weavers, servants, and other workers. Poorly paid, they lived in miserable, cramped housing and existed mainly on bread, eating as much as three pounds a day per person.

The bourgeois, or would-be nobles, were sometimes the subject of ridicule. Their desire to be noble could almost be considered comical, as this painting suggests.

A shortage of bread meant that many went hungry. The working class, especially in Paris, eventually became known as the *sans culottes* (literally, those without knee breeches) because they wore long trousers. Later they wore red woolen hats to show support for the Revolution. (This term was used during and after the Revolution.)

Life of a Peasant

The peasants of France were better off than peasants in most other European countries. But they were the poorest members of the Third Estate, and the ones who paid the most taxes. These were the "wretched" individuals whom Thomas Jefferson wrote about.

Imagine that you are a young girl, daughter of a poor peasant family in rural France in the 1700s. What is your life like?

First of all, your house is very small, with a dirt floor. Your father keeps it that way on purpose. If he made any improvements to the house, it would be worth more and he would have to pay higher taxes.

Most of your time is spent working in the fields and garden, and taking care of your younger brothers and sisters. The fields and garden don't produce much, just barely enough grain to make bread for the family. You used to have to milk the cow and put cow manure on the fields for fertilizer. But last year, the crops failed and your father sold the cow for food to feed the family through the winter. However, it wasn't quite enough, and you and your brother were sent up to the main road to beg for food.

You heard your parents talking the other day. They were upset because your brother's birthday was approaching and he was about to turn seven and that too would mean more taxes. Your family has to pay a special tax—a salt tax—for every member of your household seven and older.

On Sundays, you go to Mass at the village church. The priest is generally kind, but your parents are still angry that they have to pay a tithe of 10 percent of what they earn to the Church.

During times when there were shortages of food, French peasants suffered greatly.

Yesterday, some men came and took your father away. Your mother said it would be okay—he was going to work on the main road to Paris, which needed repair. She assured you he would be back in a few days, or maybe a week. Several other men from the village had to go too. Unfortunately, your father doesn't get paid for his work. Working for the government for free is a kind of tax called a *corvée* (/kohr*vay/), your mother says. But the family is lucky. At least they didn't take your father away to the army, which happened to some men in the next village. Most of those men never returned to their families.

At night, as you sit by the light of a candle, your mother sometimes tells stories about her childhood. She grew up in this village, and her childhood was a lot like yours is now. She endured the same hardships, and she wished for something better. You sometimes wonder if things will ever change.

Chapter 3
The Absolute Monarchs

Louis XIV—"I Am the State" Would you have wanted to be an attendant at Versailles, the court of the King Louis XIV, the great Sun King? King Louis XIV **reigned** from 1643 to 1715. If so, you would have had to follow many rules of behavior in order to find favor with King Louis.

The Big Question

How did French kings use their absolute power?

To be a successful **courtier** (/kohr*tee*ur/), you had to be willing to put up with a little discomfort. The palace contained more than two hundred guestrooms, but most were small and uncomfortable—cold in winter, hot in summer. If you were lucky, you might have caught a glimpse of the spacious living quarters of the king and queen.

Most important, you always had to keep in mind that the king was the center of the world. He was the sun, and *everything* revolved around him. You would have taken every opportunity to gain his favor.

Vocabulary

reign, v. to rule over a country as its czar, king, or queen

courtier, n. a person who serves as a friend or adviser to a ruler in his or her court

King Louis XIV was an absolute monarch.

Rules of Behavior

A **duke** who lived at Versailles explained what it took to please the king. The duke said the king liked to be flattered. People at court had to be ready with a compliment at a moment's notice— the more extravagant, the better. When servants

delivered the king's food to his table, they bowed and removed their hats. And those who attended court had to be prepared to spend money—lots of it. The king liked people around him to spend money freely and to wear expensive clothes.

People were required to follow these elaborate rules, and others, in the hope that one day they would be lucky enough to be granted one of the highest privileges the king could bestow: to hold the candle while he put on his nightgown!

An All-Powerful King

Louis XIV was the most powerful monarch in Europe and the perfect model of an absolute monarch. Louis XIV sincerely believed that he was God's representative on Earth and that he ruled by divine right. He was only twenty-three when he announced that he would be his own chief minister. This step was unheard of for a king. Kings usually let someone else do the difficult day-to-day work of running things. Louis regularly put in long workdays governing his kingdom. He believed he was more than just the ruler of the state. "I *am* the state," he boasted.

The king wanted to break the power of his nobles. He had learned his lesson early. Louis had become king when he was only four years old, in 1643. When he was ten, powerful French nobles rose up against the crown and took control of Paris. The uprising failed, but it left a mark on the young king—he learned to dislike Paris, and he became determined to keep the nobles under his thumb. He had a solution to both problems.

View of Versailles

Previous kings had lived in the royal palace of the Tuileries (/tweel*ree/) in Paris. But Louis built a magnificent palace at Versailles, eleven miles outside Paris. The palace was as long as seven football fields and was surrounded by grand gardens noted for more than a million red and yellow tulips. The palace contained more than one thousand rooms, including a library, a theater, council rooms, and spacious apartments for the king and queen.

The most striking feature of Versailles was the Hall of Mirrors. One long wall consisted of seventeen tall windows overlooking the gardens. The opposite wall held seventeen huge, gold-framed mirrors. At night, the room was lighted by thirty-two crystal chandeliers holding thousands of wax candles whose light was reflected in the mirrors. Versailles was the center of the cultural world of France and the envy of every monarch in Europe.

Versailles was the most luxurious royal home in Europe.

The Palace of Versailles was commissioned by King Louis XIV. It was the royal residence of Bourbon kings for almost one hundred years. Taxing the peasants made this luxurious lifestyle possible.

Louis insisted that the most powerful nobles—who had often rebelled against previous kings—live at least part of the year at Versailles. There he dispensed his favors, and these nobles became dependent on him. Many turned into idle, corrupt flatterers, gamblers, and gossips.

During Louis XIV's seventy-two-year reign, France became one of the most prosperous European nations and a center of European culture. Under him, art and literature flourished. However, Louis became involved in long and costly wars. When Louis XIV died in 1715, he was the most powerful ruler in Europe. But France was deeply in debt, and the people cheered at the news of his death.

Louis XV

Louis XV was the great-grandson of the Sun King, Louis XIV. Louis XV became king when he was only five years old. But Louis did not have the qualities of the Sun King. He was ineffective and more interested in having fun than

Louis XV became king of France when he was only five years old. These portraits show him as a child and as an adult.

in doing the hard work of governing. Louis claimed the role of absolute monarch, but in practice he was unable to control his ministers. During his reign of almost sixty years, France continued to become involved in costly wars, including the French and Indian War. This war, known to the French as the Seven Years' War, also caused the country to lose its colonies in North America and India.

Like his great-grandfather, Louis XV kept his court at Versailles, becoming more and more isolated from his people. As a boy, he was known as Louis the Well Beloved, but by his death, he was as thoroughly hated by the people as Louis XIV had been.

For the most part, Louis XV continued the policies of heavily taxing the poor and spending extravagantly—though in his final years, he took some steps to impose greater financial responsibilities on the French aristocracy. He knew, however, that he was leaving France in a financial crisis and that terrible problems might follow his reign.

A Young Prince

On August 23, 1754, a baby boy was born at the palace of Versailles. A courier was sent to King Louis XV, who was at another palace at the time, to announce the birth of his grandson, Louis Augustus. The courier never arrived. He was thrown from his horse and broke his neck. Perhaps it was an omen! The baby boy would grow up to be King Louis XVI, the last absolute monarch of France, who would one day die in a bloody revolution.

Louis XVI was kind and generous, but he had trouble making decisions. He was more interested in hunting than in the affairs of the country. Louis was a skilled and fearless hunter. He kept a detailed account of each hunt, totaling the number of stags, deer, and wild boar that he had killed. He also counted up, by month and year, the number of game birds that he had shot.

Once off his horse, Louis XVI was shy and awkward. At this time in history, France needed a strong and courageous leader, but Louis was neither of those things. He was an ordinary man, not especially bright or talented or bold. He was not suited to the task before him.

When Louis was fifteen, he married the beautiful fourteen-year-old Marie Antoinette, daughter of the Austrian empress, Maria Theresa. Louis adored and indulged his wife. Five years later, Louis and Marie Antoinette took the throne. "I feel like the universe is going to fall on me," Louis said when he became king. And, indeed, it eventually did.

Louis XVI married the young Austrian royal Marie Antoinette on May 16, 1770.

Chapter 4
Queen Marie Antoinette

The Future King and Queen It was a lovely summer day in June. The gilded carriage carrying the young couple drove slowly into the streets of Paris, escorted by mounted guards dressed smartly in blue coats. Cheering crowds lined the streets. People strained to get a glimpse of Louis Augustus and his pretty young wife, Marie Antoinette.

The Big Question

How might the luxurious royal lifestyle have turned the ordinary people of France against the royal family?

Vocabulary

dauphin, n. the title given to the prince who is next in line to inherit the French throne

indulge, v. to allow someone to do what they want; to spoil someone

The **dauphin** (/doh*fahn/) and the future queen of France had finally ventured from the isolated world of Versailles, where they lived in luxury and were **indulged** by their courtiers. Paris was only eleven miles away from Versailles, but the young couple had not visited the capital during the first three years of their marriage. Now the two of them came into contact with the ordinary people of Paris for the first time.

The carriage moved toward the palace of the Tuileries. The crowd surged forward as the couple stepped out of the carriage for a walk in the garden.

When Louis Augustus and Marie Antoinette married, the people of Paris celebrated with a brilliant fireworks display. But the young couple did not visit the people of Paris until three years after their wedding.

The young woman was tall and graceful. Most of all the people noticed her blue eyes. By comparison, the dauphin was awkward and shy, but he clearly adored his wife as she swept along the garden path.

A few days later, back at the palace of Versailles, Marie Antoinette wrote a letter to her mother, the Empress Maria Theresa of Austria, describing the day:

> We made our entrance into Paris. . . . The poor people . . . in spite of the taxes with which they are overwhelmed, were transported with joy at seeing us. . . . When we returned from our walk we went up to an open terrace and stayed there half an hour. I cannot describe to you, my dear mamma, the . . . joy and affection which everyone exhibited toward us. Before we withdrew we kissed our hands to the people, which gave them great pleasure. What a happy thing it is for persons in our rank to gain the love of a whole nation so cheaply. . . . I felt it thoroughly, and shall never forget it.

Louis XVI

Less than a year later, word spread like wildfire through the palace at Versailles— King Louis XV was dead! Smallpox had killed him so quickly that people were not quite prepared. The courtiers frantically searched the palace for Louis and Marie Antoinette. They would be the new king and queen, and everyone was eager to be the first to gain their favor. They were found at last, alone together, kneeling in prayer. Their prayer was overheard just as the door opened: "Protect us, O God. We are too young to reign." He was twenty; she was nineteen.

Some French people disliked the new queen simply because she was Austrian—Austria was a traditional enemy of France. But others were happy with their new monarchs. They saw the young couple as a breath of fresh air and hope for the future. King Louis XVI had simple tastes, unlike his extravagant grandfather. Marie Antoinette was considered kind and generous. Both were virtuous. The people found that a refreshing change from Louis XV.

When Louis and Marie Antoinette married (shown here), they had not expected to have to rule France at such a young age.

Dangerous Advice

Things began to go badly right away. People said that Marie Antoinette interfered in her husband's decisions about matters of state. (It wasn't true, but that didn't stop the rumors.) She had been a rich and spoiled child. Now she was determined to have her way. And her husband continued to indulge her, just as her parents had.

Allowing the court to gossip about the queen and overstate her influence was a big mistake for Louis. First of all, the courtiers realized his weakness. If they wanted something from the king, they decided that they could go through the queen. She could get anything from him.

More serious than that, though, was what happened when Louis XVI fired his grandfather's ministers. At Louis XV's direction, his ministers had begun to make reforms. Louis XV had wanted the aristocrats to pay a fair portion of taxes, which they had seldom done. The poor had no voice in the matter, but the aristocracy had a loud voice. They resisted the reforms. So when Louis XVI dismissed his grandfather's ministers, the aristocracy was happy. "He's going to be a good king," the aristocrats said among themselves. They would be able to live their lives just as before. There is debate as to whether the reforms begun by Louis XV, if continued and expanded, could have prevented the French Revolution—and saved the heads of Louis XVI and Marie Antoinette. It's impossible to say, but when Louis XVI dismissed his grandfather's advisers, these much-needed reforms stopped, and France was put back on the road to revolution.

The Extravagant Queen

Marie Antoinette's greatest weaknesses were that she liked to spend money and liked to have a good time—even when she should have been attending to her duties as queen.

She wasn't well-educated (almost no women were at that time). She wasn't interested in affairs of state, unless they were a source of gossip or scandal. The young queen hated to be bored. So she avoided boredom, even when it meant avoiding her queenly duties, such as receiving **foreign ambassadors**, attending important dinners, and so on. What she did like to do was stage dramatic productions in which she played a part.

> **Vocabulary**
>
> "foreign ambassador," (phrase) a person from another country who is an official representative of his or her government

Most of all, she liked to spend money. And her husband indulged her. He gave her an allowance that was twice what the previous queen had received. Still, she was constantly in debt.

She spent enormous amounts of money, and she liked to gamble. She often lost what would today amount to hundreds of thousands of dollars *in one night!* Her other extravagance was her wardrobe. She constantly bought clothes, spending what would today be nearly two million dollars a year.

Marie Antoinette lived a life of luxury with little understanding of how ordinary people lived. Here she is seen in the palace gardens with ladies of the royal court.

Much of that went to jewels. Even though she could wear the dazzling French crown jewels whenever she wished, she bought jewelry of her own on top of it all. She was particularly fond of the most expensive jewels of all, diamonds.

Marie Antoinette had her own personal dressmaker and beautician. She wore her hair piled up with hairpieces that reached upward of several feet. Her hairdos were sometimes decorated with miniature scenes of people, houses, and animals. In all of this, her husband continued to indulge her.

Marie Antoinette wore elaborate hairstyles.

Queen Marie as a Peasant

The most scandalous extravagance—one that earned Marie Antoinette the hatred of the French people—was *Le Petit Trianon* (/luh/puh*tee/tree*ah*non), a small mansion on the grounds of Versailles that Louis gave her. She had the grounds around the mansion enclosed with fences and gates to keep people out. (The public was allowed to walk through the rest of the gardens at Versailles.) Inside, she had a theater built alongside gardens containing a lake and river. But perhaps the most insulting thing was the little "peasant village" that she had built inside the grounds. She had people posing as peasants walking around the village, which was complete with farm animals. She herself would dress in a simple white dress and stroll through the village pretending to be a peasant. Meanwhile, the government went into debt, and people went hungry, and the real peasants suffered under the weight of taxes.

Marie Antoinette even had her own living quarters in her peasant village—though she certainly didn't live like a peasant!

Marie Antoinette and the Revolution

Many people believe that Marie Antoinette's extravagant spending and thoughtless behavior caused the French Revolution. Thomas Jefferson thought so. Jefferson spent time in France before the French Revolution and knew Marie Antoinette.

Jefferson was oversimplifying things, though: it wasn't *all* Marie Antoinette's fault. There were many factors that helped cause the French Revolution. But the behavior of Marie Antoinette did play a part. Her extravagance certainly didn't reduce the government's heavy debt, and it caused the people to hate her. She became the symbol of all that many French people thought was wrong with the monarchy and the age-old social structure in France.

A famous story is told about Marie Antoinette. It is said that when the Revolution began and the people were rioting in the streets demanding bread, she asked a servant what the uproar was about. "They are hungry, your majesty. They are rioting for bread," was the response. "Well," said Marie Antoinette, unfeelingly, "then let them eat cake."

Historians now believe this never happened. But the important point is that the people *believed* it happened, and they told and retold the story. Because of Marie Antoinette's **arrogance**, extravagance, and lack of concern about her

> ## Vocabulary
>
> **arrogance,** n. a belief or feeling of superiority

people, they were eager to believe it. And once the people were convinced that their queen was cold-hearted and cruel, their loyalty to the king and queen began to weaken.

Chapter 5
The Third Estate Revolts

A Time of Crisis In May 1789, Louis XVI had been on the throne of France for fifteen years. France was on the brink of financial collapse. The cause was not a mystery. French kings had always engaged in costly wars. The last war had been a glorious success. But debt was debt, and it was a huge problem for France.

The Big Question

What was the purpose of the meeting of the Estates-General, and why did the aristocracy and the king refuse to allow the Three Estates to meet together?

The French aristocracy would have to be forced to make changes that would help the ordinary people of France.

France had helped the Americans win their independence from the British. France's old enemy, Great Britain, had been crippled. But the war had been expensive, and France had piled an enormous new debt on top of all the old debts of the past. Plus, there was the extravagant spending at the royal court. Eventually the French government was spending half its income just to pay the **interest** on its loans. Paying off the loans themselves was impossible.

Nothing less than serious economic and political reform could fix the problem. That meant that the aristocracy would have to make some changes too. They would have to pay higher taxes. They would have to give up some of the privileges of their birth. But Louis XVI was a weak leader, and it would take a strong hand to force genuine reform on the aristocracy.

The aristocrats knew the government was in trouble and they were under threat. But they were not willing to give up something for nothing in return.

"We will agree to make some changes," they told the king, "but you must call a meeting of the **Estates-General**."

> ## Vocabulary
>
> **interest,** n. the money paid by a borrower for the use of someone else's money
>
> **Estates-General,** n. an assembly made up of representatives from France's Three Estates

The Estates-General originated in an era before kings had absolute power. Its original purpose was to give advice to the king and to approve new taxes. The nobles thought that at a meeting of the Estates-General, which hadn't met since 1614, they could push through some changes of their own. Reluctantly, Louis agreed. Neither the nobles nor the king recognized that he was opening the door to revolution.

The Estates-General Meets

On Saturday, May 2, 1789, the king sat in the dazzling Hall of Mirrors at Versailles, waiting to receive representatives from the Three Estates. The enormous doors swung open, and in marched representatives, called deputies, from the First Estate. These representatives were parish priests in black robes, and higher ranking Church leaders, such as bishops and archbishops, in their rich, elegantly embroidered robes. The king received the deputies, nodding and smiling politely at each. The deputies filed out, and the massive doors opened again to admit deputies from the Second Estate—members of the aristocracy—the nobility. The members were splendidly dressed in satin suits with lace cuffs, plumed hats, silver vests, and brilliantly colored silk cloaks, with their swords hanging at their sides. Again, the king received them graciously.

Outside the hall waited deputies of the Third Estate—the commoners. The commoners were dressed in plain, simple clothes. They waited three hours before being received—and then not in the Hall of Mirrors but in a smaller room, where they marched in single file past a solemn and unsmiling king. The deputies of the Third Estate could see that they would have to fight for real change.

According to the ancient rules of the Estates-General, each of the Three Estates met separately to vote on a proposal. Then each Estate cast one vote based on the decision of its members. In that way, the First and Second Estates, which usually had a common interest in preserving their privileges, dominated the Estates-General.

Now the Third Estate wanted to change the rules so that it would have a real voice in the reform. Deputies knew that the nobility and clergy wanted to keep the rights and privileges that they had always had under the *ancien régime*. But the Third Estate had more deputies than the other two Estates combined. The deputies knew that some of the clergy, especially parish priests, and even a few members of the nobility, were sympathetic to their problem. The Third Estate wanted all Three Estates to meet together, with each deputy casting one vote. If this happened, the Third Estate could easily control the outcome of the voting. Naturally the nobles objected, and the king sided with them. Each Estate was assigned a separate meeting hall.

The ordinary person in France at this time felt the taxes imposed on them by the king and the nobility were overwhelmingly unfair.

A National Assembly Is Created

In the large meeting hall assigned to the Third Estate, the deputies wandered around, getting acquainted with one another. The public was admitted to the hall, and they crowded around the deputies, offering advice and support.

Over the next few days, the meetings were noisy and confusing. Some deputies were willing to settle for small changes, but others argued for nothing less than a constitution and the end of the *ancien régime*. A pamphlet written by a clergyman named Abbé Sieyès (/ab*ay/see*aye*yes/) created a stir. Sieyès was known as a champion of the poor. He had a weak voice and was not an effective public speaker, so he wrote a pamphlet to express his ideas about the Third Estate. The pamphlet was read by many people and often quoted during arguments for reform:

What is the Third Estate? Everything!

What has it been up to now in the political order? Nothing!

What does it demand? To become something!

By the end of the month, all they could agree on was that they should ask deputies from the First Estate to join them in their meeting hall. The deputies sent a **delegation** to the hall where the clergy were meeting.

"The gentlemen of the commons," announced the leader of the delegation in solemn tones, "invite the gentlemen of the clergy, in the name of the God of Peace and for the national interest, to meet them in their hall to consult upon the means of bringing about the concord (agreement) which is so vital at this moment for the public welfare."

Some clergy were excited at the announcement and would have gone immediately. But other, more conservative clergymen—mostly those higher in the Church who came from noble families—wanted to discuss the proposal first before agreeing to meet.

M. L'ABBÉ SEYÈS
Député de Paris, à l'Assemblée Nationale
Ennemi du mensonge et de l'ambition,
Il sçut de la vertu relever l'édifice ;
Et de ses intérêts le noble sacrifice
Assure de nos Loix la réformation.

Abbé Sieyès wrote a powerful pamphlet, *What Is The Third Estate?,* which stirred the bourgeois to revolt.

The delegation went back to their meeting hall to wait. They were prepared to remain in session until an answer was received. Hours passed, and the delegation was sent again to repeat the invitation. Still no answer. Days passed. Finally, on June 13, three priests appeared at the door of the meeting hall. They wanted to join with the deputies of the Third Estate. Inside the hall the deputies cheered, clapped, and embraced the priests and one another with tears in their eyes. Over the next few days, more priests followed, and then more.

The Third Estate was ready now to begin its real work. Abbé Sieyès reminded the deputies that the Third Estate represented 98 percent of the population. He suggested a new name: the National Assembly. The suggestion raised an uproar in the hall. Immediately, a debate over the name raged furiously, with as many as one hundred deputies all shouting at once. To take that name would mean that the Third Estate intended to represent the whole nation and take on the responsibility for reform. There would be no going back. The debate continued into the night, while outside a summer thunderstorm raged.

The next morning, June 17, 1789, the rain ended and the sky was clear. The deputies met again and voted. The name, National Assembly, was agreed upon by a vote of 491 to 89. When news of the vote reached the meeting of the First Estate, they took a vote as well and agreed to join the new National Assembly. Eventually, the nobles would also join them.

The Tennis Court Oath

The king was outraged when he heard the news, and so the next day, when deputies of the National Assembly arrived at their meeting hall, they found the doors locked. The king plotted to hold a separate meeting of the Three Estates and declare the actions of the Third Estate illegal. He intended to keep the commoners in their place. But the deputies would not back down.

Someone suggested that they meet at a nearby building that housed the royal indoor tennis courts. The deputies crowded into the building, while outside a crowd gathered shouting, *"Vive l'assemblée!"* (/veeve/lah*sem*blay/), "Long live the assembly!"

Inside, deputies debated moving their meeting to Paris, where they would have the protection of the people. Then a young deputy rose to speak. He urged them not to move to Paris, but instead to all take an oath to stay together, to stay persistent in their goal, and never to separate until they had written a constitution.

Then, Jean-Sylvain Bailly (/zhahn/seal*vahn/bay*ee), who had been chosen to lead the meeting, stood on a table made from a door ripped off its hinges. One by one, the deputies came forward, arms raised in salute, and signed the oath. This came to be known as the Tennis Court Oath. Every deputy but one signed. A constitution would be written. The French Revolution had begun.

This painting by artist Jacques-Louis David depicts the famous scene of the deputies taking the Tennis Court Oath as a heroic and glorious moment—the beginning of the Revolution.

Chapter 6
A Time of Violence

The Stage Is Set for Violence

King Louis XVI was angry that the new National Assembly refused to disband— and he was nervous, so nervous that he no longer trusted his own French troops. He had his Swiss Guards brought from France's borders to the outskirts of Paris to protect him.

The Big Question

What sequence of events caused people to storm the Bastille, and why did the unrest spread?

The people of Paris and the deputies of the National Assembly were alarmed. Rumors started to fly. What was the king planning to do with these troops? Would he arrest the deputies of the Third Estate just when they thought they might make some changes, maybe get a little freedom and relief from the overwhelming tax burdens?

Was the king going to stop them now? On July 8, one of the strongest leaders of the new assembly spoke out angrily. He said that all these troops arriving in Paris every day were "preparations for war." The members of the assembly should not sit quietly and watch this happen, he argued.

The Swiss Guards were employed by European royal courts when needed.

King Louis XVI failed to recognize that certain changes were inevitable.

En 1786,
Le Roi LOUIS XV
donna son portrait
AUMONT DE LA MILL
Intendant général des Ponts et Chau

In Paris, the working class—the *sans culottes*—grew more alarmed and angry. Because of the failing economy, one hundred fifty thousand Parisians (out of a population of six hundred thousand) were out of work. Bread had been in short supply for several months, and prices had risen so high that a single loaf cost as much as a half day's pay. Because of these outrageous prices, many people went hungry. Working people were convinced that aristocrats and grain suppliers were withholding grain to force the price of bread even higher.

Then, on July 12, the king made another mistake—a big one. He fired his **finance minister**, Jacques (/zhahk/) Necker, who had encouraged Louis to give in to the Third Estate's demands.

Now the king had gotten rid of Necker and was organizing his troops. People thought that the king, under the influence of the queen and the nobles at court, would use force to disband the National Assembly and take back all that they had gained.

With such rumors flying around, it's no wonder that angry mobs roamed the streets, breaking into shops, looting and grabbing weapons, threatening the homes of the wealthy, and stealing bread from bakeries. The stage was set for the first and most famous outbreak of violence of the French Revolution.

The working people of Paris believed that Necker was their ally. They believed that only he could control the price of bread, make tax reforms, and save the country from financial disaster.

To the Bastille!

The Bastille (/ba*stee*yuh/) was an old fortress from the 1300s, with stone walls five feet thick and eight stone towers. A moat surrounded the outer wall; a drawbridge led to the entrance. An inner court was protected by a second moat and drawbridge. The Bastille was the object of legend and mystery to most Parisians. It was rumored that men were chained in secret dungeons. Actually, the Bastille held only seven prisoners on July 14, 1789. There were even plans to have the prison demolished. But to Parisians, it represented the tyranny of the Bourbon kings.

Bernard de Launay (/loh*nay/), governor of the Bastille, was according to one of his officers, "without much knowledge of military affairs, without experience, and without much courage."

On the morning of July 14, the sky was heavy with dark rain clouds. Launay walked the Bastille's ramparts, the tops of the high walls, thinking about the reports he had heard of riots throughout the city overnight.

The Bastille was manned with eighty-two elderly soldiers, plus thirty-two Swiss Guards. Stockpiled inside were 250 barrels of gunpowder that had been moved to the Bastille for safekeeping. There were numerous cannons and smaller guns. The drawbridges were pulled closed. Launay was ready for trouble, or so he thought.

That morning, rioters had broken into the storage facility where the army's weapons were kept. The crowd took thirty thousand muskets and carried off the cannons stored there. But they had no gunpowder and only a few bullets. Then the rioters learned that the gunpowder had been moved to the Bastille. The shout went up: "To the Bastille! To the Bastille!" From his window in the Bastille, Launay could hear the noisy mob approaching.

When the rioters arrived at the Bastille, they saw walls bristling with cannons. They were convinced that the cannons were going to be used to attack the city, not simply to defend the Bastille.

An official delegation went to Launay to ask him to remove the cannons from the walls and to hand over the fortress to a group of citizen soldiers. Launay agreed to remove the cannons, but he refused to surrender the Bastille.

As news of the crisis spread, more and more *sans culottes* joined the crowd outside the Bastille. Several men broke the pulleys holding the drawbridges, and the crowd surged into the courtyard where there was a second set of drawbridges. Shots rang out from the crowd and from the soldiers on the ramparts. The crowd shouted, "Down with the bridges!"

Eventually, realizing that resistance was useless, Launay opened the gates. Crowds of armed men immediately surged into the prison, taking the soldiers and Swiss Guards captive and freeing the seven prisoners.

Launay was taken prisoner, but his guards could not protect him from the angry mob. Before he could reach safety, Launay was brutally killed, along with another defender. Many people were horrified at the savagery of the mob. But to many, the fall of the Bastille was the true beginning of the Revolution.

The few prisoners that were held at the Bastille were set free.

The Bastille, which had symbolized the absolute power of the French kings, fell on July 14, 1789. Within one year, it was completely torn down and its bricks sold as souvenirs.

The morning after the fall of the Bastille, King Louis was awakened early with the news. "Is this a rebellion?" he asked the official who had brought him the news.

"No sire, this is a revolution," was the now famous reply. Strangely, the king wrote the following journal entry for the day: *"Rien,"* meaning "nothing."

The Great Fear

Necker, the finance minister whose firing had triggered the riots, was returned to office two days later. But rioting and violence continued. In Paris, two of the king's officials were attacked and killed by a mob in a particularly gruesome manner.

The violence spread throughout the countryside. A poor harvest in 1788 had caused a shortage of grain. Bread was in short supply in the countryside as well as in the cities. Peasants attacked millers who were accused of hoarding grain. They destroyed fences and walls on estates, killing animals in the private forests of the nobility. They broke into the manors where nobles lived. Sometimes they killed the manor lord and his family. Some nobles decided to flee France and settle in other countries. They were called *émigrés* (/aye*mih*grays/).

As the violence continued, a period of confusion and panic known as the Great Fear swept the countryside. Wild rumors spread that bands of violent ruffians—British troops or Spanish troops—in the pay of the nobility, were roaming the countryside, burning crops and murdering peasants. In a panic, peasants armed themselves with whatever they could find—knives, pitchforks, hoes. They hid in the forest or in caves.

In villages and towns in France, people took to the streets. Many rioted and stole food. They challenged local authorities.

When the murdering gangs failed to materialize, the fear passed as quickly as it had appeared. But the people continued rioting. In villages, the king's officials abandoned their offices. They were replaced with middle-class mayors and officials friendly to the Revolution. Central authority was breaking down. The militia did not help because most of its members sympathized with the rioters.

In Versailles, the National Assembly was in session working on reforms and a constitution. News of the summer's riots and looting alarmed the deputies. A duke who was one of the richest nobles of the land spoke to the assembly:

"In several **provinces** the whole people form a kind of league for the destruction of the manor houses, the ravaging of the lands, and especially for the seizure of the **archives** where the **title deeds** to feudal properties are kept. It seeks to throw off at last a **yoke** that has for many centuries weighted it down."

The question that faced the National Assembly now was what to do about the violence.

Chapter 7
Toward a New Government

The Night of August 4 From all across France, reports of violence poured into the hall where deputies of the National Assembly were meeting. They knew that to have a new, stable government in France, they had to restore order. But how?

The Big Question

How significant was the Declaration of the Rights of Man, and what prompted the women's march to Versailles?

Several deputies said the only way to remove the cause of the rioting would be to give up some of the nobility's ancient feudal privileges. One of the deputies said that all people should pay taxes according to their incomes. This meant that the nobility would pay their fair share of taxes for the first time. Another deputy suggested that peasants should be allowed to hunt in their manor lord's forest. A third deputy said that ordinary citizens should be allowed to hold public offices and positions in the army that were reserved for the nobility.

An excited public watched from the observation balcony as one by one the deputies stood up to name old feudal rights to be given up. The excitement grew to a frenzy—a "contagion of sentimental feeling," as one observer called it—as the deputies cried to outdo one another in giving up ancient feudal claims. Clergy gave up the right to tithes; lords gave up the right to collect land rents.

The decisions made at the National Assembly meeting on August 4, 1789, began the transformation of France from a feudal society to a modern nation.

One of the more conservative deputies tried to stop the proceedings. He passed a note to the president of the assembly that read, "Suspend the session. They have all gone quite mad."

But the session continued through the night. By daylight, the rights and privileges of the French feudal system of the *ancien régime* had been swept away. Some of the changes were later modified, but the door was opened for a new system of government and a constitution.

The Declaration of the Rights of Man

The National Assembly was ready to begin framing a constitution for the new nation.

Some deputies argued that a strong constitution must be based on the rights of man, and must protect these rights, which are rights granted to all men by **natural law**.

Some deputies nodded in agreement. Yes, they must have a Bill of Rights, like the English had passed in 1689 and like the Bill of Rights the American Congress was working on. The ideas of freedom and equality must be stated as the basis for the constitution.

Other deputies disagreed. It works for the Americans and the British, they said, because they have a history of freedom. But the people of France have lived for centuries under a feudal system. They might not yet be ready for equality.

The two sides continued to debate, but in the end, the supporters of natural rights won. On August 27, 1789, the National Assembly issued the Declaration of the Rights of Man.

The first article of the Declaration read, "Men are born and remain free and equal in rights."

"These rights are liberty, property, security, and resistance to oppression," read the second article.

DÉCLARATION DES DROITS DE L'HOMME ET DU CITOYEN,
Décrétés par l'Assemblée Nationale dans les séances des 20, 21, 23, 24 et 26 août 1789, acceptés par le Roi.

PRÉAMBULE

LES représentans du peuple François, constitués en assemblée nationale, considérant que l'ignorance, l'oubli ou le mépris des droits de l'homme sont les seules causes des malheurs publics et de la corruption des gouvernemens, ont résolu d'exposer dans une déclaration solemnelle, les droits naturels, inaliénables et sacrés de l'homme, afin que cette déclaration, constamment présente a tous les membres du corps social, leur rappelle sans cesse leurs droits et leurs devoirs, afin que les actes du pouvoir legislatif et ceux du pouvoir exécutif, pouvant être à chaque instant comparés avec le but de toute institution politique, en soient plus respectés, afin que les reclamations des citoyens, fondées désormais sur des principes simples et incontestables, tournent toujours au maintien de la constitution et du bonheur de tous.

EN conséquence, l'assemblée nationale reconnoit et déclare, en presence et sous les auspices de l'Etre suprême les droits suivans de l'homme et du citoyen.

ARTICLE PREMIER

LES hommes naissent et demeurent libres et égaux en droits. les distinctions sociales ne peuvent être fondées que sur l'utilité commune.

II.

LE but de toute association politique est la conservation des droits naturels et imprescriptibles de l'homme; ces droits sont la liberté, la propriété, la sûreté, et la résistance à l'oppression.

III.

LE principe de toute souveraineté réside essentiellement dans la nation, nul corps, nul individu ne peut exercer d'autorité qui n'en émane expressément.

IV.

LA liberté consiste a pouvoir faire tout ce qui ne nuit pas à autrui. Ainsi, l'exercice des droits naturels de chaque homme, n'a de bornes que celles qui assurent aux autres membres de la société la jouissance de ces mêmes droits; ces bornes ne peuvent être déterminées que par la loi.

V.

LA loi n'a le droit de défendre que les actions nuisibles à la société. Tout ce qui n'est pas défendu par la loi ne peut être empêché. et nul ne peut être contraint à faire ce qu'elle n'ordonne pas.

VI.

LA loi est l'expression de la volonté générale; tous les citoyens ont droit de concourir personnellement, ou par leurs représentans, à sa formation. elle doit être la même pour tous, soit qu'elle protege, soit qu'elle punisse. Tous les citoyens étant égaux a ses yeux, sont également admissibles à toutes dignités, places et emplois publics, selon leur capacité, et sans autres distinction que celles de leurs vertus et de leurs talens.

VII.

NUL homme ne peut être accusé, arrêté ni détenu que dans les cas déterminés par la loi, et selon les formes qu'elle a prescrites, ceux qui sollicitent, expédient, exécutent ou font exécuter des ordres arbitraires, doivent être punis; mais tout citoyen appelé ou saisi en vertu de la loi, doit obéir à l'instant, il se rend coupable par la résistance.

VIII.

LA loi ne doit établir que des peines strictement et évidemment nécessaire, et nul ne peut être puni qu'en vertu d'une loi établie et promulguée antérieurement au délit, et légalement appliquée.

IX.

TOUT homme étant présumé innocent jusqu'à ce qu'il ait été déclaré coupable, s'il est jugé indispensable de l'arrêter, toute rigueur qui ne serait pas nécessaire pour s'assurer de sa personne doit être sévèrement réprimée par la loi.

X.

NUL ne doit être inquiété pour ses opinions, mêmes religieuses pourvu que leur manifestation ne trouble pas l'ordre public établi par la loi.

XI.

LA libre communication des pensées et des opinions est un des droits les plus precieux de l'homme; tout citoyen peut dont parler écrire, imprimer librement; sauf à répondre de l'abus de cette liberté dans les cas déterminés par la loi.

XII.

LA garantie des droits de l'homme et du citoyen nécessite une force publique; cette force est donc instituée pour l'avantage de tous, et non pour l'utilité particuliere de ceux a qui elle est confiée.

XIII.

POUR l'entretien de la force publique, et pour les dépenses d'administration, une contribution commune est indispensable; elle doit être également répartie entre les citoyens en raison de leurs facultées.

XIV.

LES citoyens ont le droit de constater par eux même ou par leurs représentans, la nécessité de la contribution publique, de la consentir librement, d'en suivre l'emploi, et d'en déterminer la quotité, l'assiette, le recouvrement et la durée.

XV.

LA société a le droit de demander compte a tout agent public de son administration.

XVI.

TOUTE société, dans laquelle la garantie des droits n'est pas assurée, ni la séparation des pouvoirs déterminée, n'a point de constitution.

XVII.

LES propriétés étant un droit inviolable et sacré, nul ne peut en être privé, si ce n'est lorsque la nécessité publique, légalement constatée, l'exige evidemment, et sous la condition d'une juste et préalable indemnité.

AUX REPRESENTANS DU PEUPLE FRANCOIS

The Declaration of the Rights of Man was not only about the rights of French citizens—it claimed that *all* people had natural rights.

Other articles in the Declaration gave citizens freedom of speech, freedom of religion, and equal justice. The Declaration promised that no one would receive special privileges and that everyone would have equality before the law.

The Declaration also stated that the people had the right to have a say in how they would be governed. The absolute monarchy was abolished. After much debate, they decided that the king could remain on the throne, but he would no longer have absolute power.

The deputies were finally ready to begin drafting a constitution. But they still had many disagreements. For instance, exactly how much power should the king have? These debates were going on when once again, the poor people spoke.

Women March to Versailles

In Paris, the shortage of bread was reaching a crisis. Fighting broke out in bread lines; bakers were threatened with hanging.

Among the poor working classes, women were the ones in charge of getting the daily supply of bread. They also often worked for wages. Because of this, women especially felt the burden of the shortage of bread and of the widespread unemployment.

On October 5, 1789, a rough and angry crowd of women gathered at city hall demanding bread. They were told they would have to see the king, so the crowd of women began the long hike to Versailles. Some were well-dressed bourgeois women who genuinely believed that if the king knew what was happening to the people, he would help solve the problem. They marched side by side with ordinary women. Some of the women who marched were armed with pikes; some tore down shop signs; some criticized the queen.

Along the way, other women joined them. The crowd eventually grew to more than six thousand. Many of the women carried broomsticks and kitchen knives. It had begun to rain, and by the time they reached Versailles in the late afternoon, they were soaked and muddy.

In Paris, a **citizens' militia**, or National Guard, had been formed after the fall of the Bastille. It was commanded by the Marquis de Lafayette—the

> ### Vocabulary
> **"citizens' militia,"** (phrase) an army composed of the people of a nation rather than of soldiers

The women who protested wanted the king to come to Paris to solve the problem of the shortage of bread. Others wanted the king in Paris so they could keep an eye on him.

same Lafayette who had fought beside George Washington in the American Revolution. When the National Guard heard the news of the women's march, they demanded that Lafayette lead them to Versailles to bring the king back to Paris to face the protesters.

By this time, the women had arrived at Versailles and pushed into the hall where the National Assembly was meeting. The women shouted at the deputies from the galleries lining the meeting hall. As deputies tried to continue debating the constitution, one woman shouted down at them: "Who's that talking down there? Make the chatterbox shut up. That's not the point: the point is that we want bread!"

Finally, a delegation of six women was allowed to meet with the king. "Sire, we want bread," said the spokeswoman of the group. "You know my heart," answered the king. "I will order all the bread in Versailles to be collected and given to you." The king thought that was the end of the crisis and went to bed.

Sometime around six o'clock the next morning, the queen was awakened by shouting in the rooms below her. A mob of women had broken into the palace, and they were looking for her. Two of the queen's bodyguards were killed as they tried to stop the mob. "We want to cut off her head," they screamed.

The terrified queen leaped out of bed and fled through a hidden staircase to the king's rooms. When the mob reached the queen's empty bedroom, they slashed her bedsheets with knives.

Lafayette's men arrived and managed to clear the palace of the rioters, but the crowd had gathered in the courtyard, where they shouted, "The king to Paris! The king to Paris!"

Finally, the king appeared on his balcony overlooking the rowdy crowd in the courtyard below. "My friends," he announced, "I will go to Paris with my wife and children." The queen and the royal children also appeared before the crowd.

That afternoon, they set out for Paris through the mud and rain. The National Guard rode in front of the coach that carried the king and queen and their children, while Lafayette himself rode beside the coach. The crowd of women walked alongside the carriage, carrying pikes with the heads of the queen's guards. Some of the women shouted insults at the queen, and others chanted, "We are bringing the baker, the baker's wife, and the baker's boy— now we shall have bread!"

The royal family was forced to leave Versailles and was taken to Paris.

After six long hours, the royal family reached Paris and was taken to the Tuileries. Dust and cobwebs filled the rooms—very different from the magnificent palace at Versailles. But neither the king, nor queen, nor their son would ever see Versailles again. Their daughter would survive the events that were about to occur, but would spend much of her remaining life outside of France.

Reforms and the Constitution

The deputies of the National Assembly followed the king to Paris and began announcing a series of reforms that turned France upside down. In its first eighteen months, the assembly passed laws that formed the basis of a new constitution.

The deputies created a limited **constitutional monarchy**; the assembly would make the laws, and the king and his ministers were responsible for enforcing them.

> **Vocabulary**
>
> **constitutional monarchy,** n. government by a king or queen whose power is limited by a constitution

The government took over the lands of the Catholic Church and sold them to pay off its heavy debts. The assembly decided that clergy would be elected by the voters—property-owning males—and paid by the state; thus, priests became elected state officials. This angered many religious believers, turning them against the Revolution.

The king agreed to approve both the Declaration of the Rights of Man and the constitution. Many people thought that the Revolution was completed, but they were wrong—another, more violent, upheaval was coming.

Chapter 8
From Monarchy to Republic

Escape! Shortly after midnight on June 21, 1791, a plump man in dark clothes passed through the palace gates of the Tuileries. The guard paid little attention; he had seen a duke leave at the same time every night. But this night it was different. This night, the man in dark clothes was actually the king of France in disguise!

The Big Question

What happened to the royal family?

Once through the gate, the king entered a waiting carriage. Inside were two women and two children: the king's sister, his two children (his daughter, and his son dressed as a little girl), and the children's governess. In the dim light, another woman approached the carriage. It was Marie Antoinette, dressed in a simple dress and hat.

The royal family was attempting to escape to Austria. There, the queen's brother, the Austrian emperor, might be persuaded to invade France and restore the monarchy to its old powers.

Their plans failed. They were discovered when they reached the town of Varennes (/vah*ren/) by a man who recognized the king from his image on French money. The king and his family were brought back to Paris in humiliation. Soldiers of the National Guard lined the streets of Paris, their muskets reversed as if for a funeral. Huge crowds watched the passing carriage, but they were silent.

King Louis and his family failed to escape France and were forced to return to Paris.

All had read the official notices that had been posted, warning the people: "Whoever applauds the king shall be flogged [whipped]; whoever insults him shall be hanged."

Now the king had lost not only the limited power he had as a constitutional monarch but also the love and trust of his people. He and his family would now be prisoners in the palace of the Tuileries.

A New Legislative Assembly

In September 1791, the National Assembly finished its job and stepped down. A new **Legislative Assembly** took its place, composed of younger men with different ideas. However, the old problems remained—jobs and bread were still in short supply—and the people were getting angry once again.

The Legislative Assembly held its meetings in the royal riding school in the gardens of the Tuileries, which now housed the king. In the center of the hall sat the president.

The new deputies of the assembly were solid members of the middle class and included many lawyers, but they were deeply divided into two factions, which held conflicting ideas. Some deputies were conservatives who wanted to keep the limited monarchy. Other deputies were radicals who wanted to get rid of the king and set up a **republic**.

> ### Vocabulary
>
> **Legislative Assembly,** n. a group of representatives with the power to make laws for the country
>
> **republic,** n. a government in which people elect representatives to rule for them

The radicals sat to the left of the president, and the conservatives sat to his right. Soon people began to refer to deputies as "left-wingers" or "right-wingers." Elsewhere in France, there were some people whose views were even more extreme than the views of the deputies in the Legislative Assembly. On the left, there were some extreme radicals who wanted to sweep away all of the old rules and traditions, and establish complete equality and democracy. On the extreme right, there were conservatives who wanted to go back to the absolute monarchy. By this time, however, most conservatives had left the country.

France at War

The Austrian emperor, Leopold II, who was also Marie Antoinette's brother, supported the extreme right-wingers. He did not support the Revolution in France—after all, it set a bad example. Other Europeans might start wanting liberty and equality too, and then what would happen to European monarchs like him? And, revolution could spread to European colonies too. Then what would happen? Indeed revolution did spread beyond Europe. On August 22, 1791, fifty thousand enslaved workers rose up on a French colonial island in the Caribbean called St. Domingue. With its sugar plantations, this island was the richest Caribbean colony. After the revolt, this island would be renamed Haiti, and it would become the first black republic in the world.

Marie Antoinette's brother, Leopold II, was the emperor of Austria.

When Austria threatened to attack France, the radicals in the assembly responded with enthusiasm. They felt this would give France an opportunity to spread its revolutionary ideals: liberty—freedom of speech, religion, the press, and so on; equality—all citizens equal under the law, no special privileges for any one group; fraternity—the comradeship of all French citizens working together for the good of France.

"France must rise to the full height of her mission!" shouted one deputy.

"Yes, yes!" shouted the others. And then they declared war on Austria.

The war went badly for France. "I am not able to understand," raged Lafayette, "how we could ever get into war without the slightest preparation!"

The poorly trained soldiers fled at the sight of the well-equipped, well-trained armies of the enemy. Their flight left the road to Paris open. Rumors spread wildly through Paris. The king and queen are traitors! They have betrayed us to the enemy! How else could the French army be so easily beaten? Once again, the *sans culottes* turned to violence.

Early in the morning of August 10, 1792, the king and queen, who had been awake all night, listened to the church bells ring an ominous alarm. They knew that something terrible was about to happen. The loyal Swiss Guards stood by, ready to defend the Tuileries. Then news came—the *sans culottes*

The French aristocrat Marquis de Lafayette

had taken over the city government, and a mob was rapidly approaching the Tuileries.

When the mob broke through the heavy oak gates, the palace defenders were ready. They fired muskets and cannons, and the mob retreated. But then there was a new sound—not a mob, but marching feet. It was the militia from the provinces, mainly from the southern province of Marseilles (/mar*say/). These were rough and ragged men who had marched all the way to Paris to join the fight against the Austrians. Along the way, they sang a song, "The Marseillaise" (/mahr*say*yez/), that later would become the French national anthem. The troops were intent on dethroning the king.

Despite heroic efforts by the palace guards, the militia and mob forced their way into the palace. Meanwhile, a deputy of the National Assembly was with the royal family, ready to take them to safety.

"Look, sire!" he cried, as he pointed out the window. "A whole people are advancing! If the palace must fall, let it fall; but let the crown be saved."

The king and his family hurried through the back of the palace and made their way across the gardens to seek protection of the Legislative Assembly, which was meeting in the riding school. But the assembly could not protect them.

Meanwhile, the mob burst into the palace and slaughtered five hundred members of the Swiss Guards. Then they killed anyone else they could find in the palace—cooks, maids, and servants—and went from room to room, looting and destroying. More than one thousand people perished.

The violence marked the end of the monarchy. The king and his family were taken as prisoners to the Temple, a medieval fortress. The coachmen drove slowly so people in the streets could witness the royal family on its nightmare journey to prison.

Even the Tuileries, the palace that had become a prison, was no longer safe for the royal family.

In September, a new and far more radical legislative assembly, the National Convention, was elected. It would soon decide the fate of King Louis XVI and Queen Marie Antoinette.

The Death of the King

On September 22, 1792, the National Convention declared France a republic and announced the end of the monarchy. Now Louis was harmless and had no power. Stripped of his crown and title, he was to be known as Louis Capet (/ka*pay/). The revolutionaries were not sure what to do with him, though. They spent hours debating his fate.

"The king must be killed," declared the young, elegant—but cruel—deputy, Antoine de Saint-Just (/an*twahn/duh/sahn*zhoost/). "Royalty is an eternal crime. The king must not have a long trial. He must be killed."

"But what was his crime?" others asked. "Should a man be killed just because he was born a king?"

Despite these objections, the king was put on trial. In the convention, one delegate argued against the trial: "I am tired of my part of **despotism**—tormented by the tyranny I am forced to exercise."

But the trial went on, and Louis was found guilty of conspiracy against the nation. What would be his punishment? Imprisonment? Banishment?

After three days of debate, the vote was taken and the verdict was announced: the king must die! The most shocking vote in favor of the death penalty was cast by the former Duke of Orléans, a cousin of Louis who had changed his name to Philippe Égalité (/fih*leep/ aye*gal*ee*tay/), or Philip Equality. Later, when the Revolution swirled out of control, Philippe Egalité would himself be executed.

On January 21, 1793, Louis, the descendant of Bourbon kings who had ruled France for centuries, was driven in a carriage to the **guillotine** (/gee*yuh*teen/). Weak during life, he approached his death with dignity and high courage. Louis calmly climbed the steps to the guillotine, his priest beside him; he placed his head beneath the heavy blade that hung high above him.

He began to speak: "I die innocent . . .," but a roll of drums drowned out his words. The blade fell and the crowd cheered, "Long live the Republic!" Some formed a human chain that danced around the guillotine singing "The Marseillaise."

The king was dead, and the queen would soon follow in his footsteps.

The Fate of the Queen

On the morning of October 16, 1793, Marie Antoinette dressed herself for the last time. She wore a white dress, stockings, and silk shoes. Guards escorted her from her dark prison cell and placed her in an open cart for the long ride to the guillotine. She too had been tried, convicted, and sentenced to death. The only reminder that she had been a queen was in her bearing. She held her head high, but gone was the sparkling, lovely Marie Antoinette. Here was a tired woman, dressed in plain clothing more fit for a chambermaid.

As she climbed the steps to the guillotine, some observers stated that she accidentally stepped on her executioner's foot and said, "Pardon me, Sir. I meant not to do it." Those, it is claimed by some, were her last words.

King Louis XVI was sent to the guillotine. His execution horrified many Europeans who opposed the French Revolution.

Marie Antoinette, the queen who had lived a life of luxury, was taken to her death in a cart.

Chapter 9
Religion, Culture, and Art

Wiping Out the Old Regime The radical leaders of the French Revolution wanted to destroy everything that they hated about the *ancien régime* and reform virtually every aspect of French life. Many of the revolutionary leaders shared Voltaire's dislike for the Roman Catholic Church.

The Big Question

Why do you think the revolutionaries wanted to change so much of French society?

During the French Revolution, land owned by the Catholic Church was taken away.

These leaders doubted the Church's religious doctrines. They hated the wealthy Church leaders, such as bishops, who had helped strengthen the old regime. So it was no surprise that the Church soon came under attack.

The revolutionaries had already begun stripping away the power of the Catholic Church. They took all the Church's land and sold it. They tried to transform the Roman Catholic Church into a French national church. They forced priests to take an oath of loyalty declaring their support for the new constitution. Priests who refused (and there were many) were driven out of their parishes and treated as enemies of the state.

These actions angered many of the Catholics in France. Not only parish priests and higher Church officials, but also ordinary people began to turn against the Revolution. Even the pope condemned the Revolution.

The Attack on the Church

After the king's execution, the revolutionaries became even more hostile toward the Church. Anti-Church radicals took over the **cathedral** of Notre-Dame, tore out statues of the saints, and replaced them with statues of Voltaire and Rousseau.

> **Vocabulary**
>
> **cathedral,** n. the bishop's church; any large and important church
>
> **civic,** adj. relating to a city, citizen, or community

Radical revolutionary leaders decided that France needed to replace the old Christian religion with a new faith. They announced a Festival of the Supreme Being to introduce the people of France to the new **civic** religion.

Paris was excited. Houses were decorated with flowers and colors of the Revolution. The best artists in France worked to prepare for the festival. In the garden of the Tuileries, thousands gathered to hear revolutionaries praise the Supreme Being. One leader, Maximilien Robespierre (/rohbz*pee*air/), supported such beliefs.

Even though Notre-Dame Cathedral was attacked and looted during the French Revolution, it still stands today in the center of Paris. It remains a place of worship for French Catholics.

A New Calendar

Imagine telling someone that your birthday is the 18th of Floreal, Year II. According to the new calendar of the Revolution, that was the new name for what used to be called May 7, 1794. The most extreme of the French revolutionaries wanted to get rid of all traces of Christianity. Because the old calendar counted dates from the birth of Jesus Christ, they decided to abolish it. They invented a new calendar—one that was based on the start of the French Revolution. The first day of Year I was September 22, 1792, the day after the National Convention took power.

The new calendar eliminated all of the inconsistencies of the old calendar. There were now twelve months, each thirty days long. Each month was divided into three ten-day weeks. A festival honoring the *sans culottes* was celebrated during the last five days of each year. The months were named

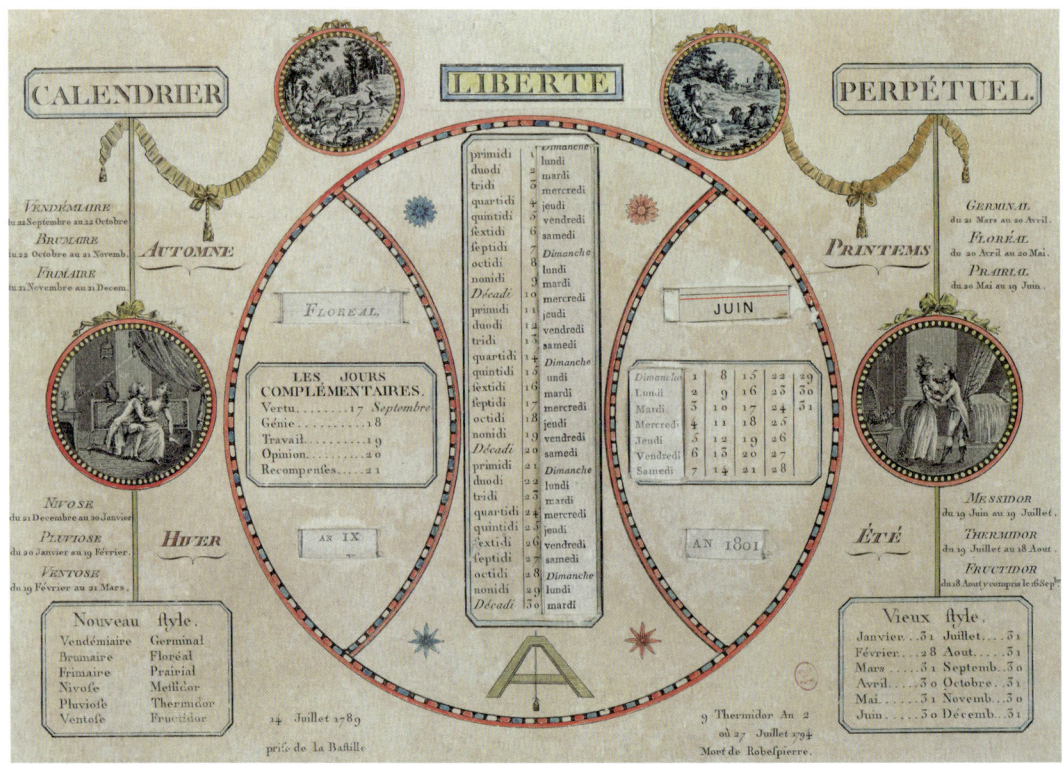

The revolutionaries rejected the Gregorian calendar that was introduced in the late 1500s and created their own calendar.

for natural events during seasons. For example, Floreal was the month of flowers; the month of Thermidor (heat) was from July 19 to August 17.

The Metric System

Also introduced at this time was a new system of weights and measures—the metric system. This system featuring liters, meters, and kilograms, was created by French scientists. Up until this point, there had been many different ways of measuring and weighing things in various parts of France.

New Styles in Clothing and Speech

Clothing styles also changed dramatically during the Revolution. Gone were the tall, powdered wigs and elaborate, heavy dresses of the *ancien régime.* Men now wore plain clothes with little decoration. Women wore short, simple hairdos and soft cotton dresses and sandals, imitating the simpler fashions of ancient Greece. The new styles reflected the modesty and virtue that were expected in the new republic.

During the *ancien régime*, people had addressed one another as *monsieur* (/muhs*yuhr/) (for a man), *madame* (/muh*dam/) (a married woman), or *mademoiselle* (/mad*mwah*zel/) (an unmarried woman). In the new republic, people had to use the terms *citizen* and citoyen (/sit*woy*yeh/) or citoyenne (/sit*woy*yehn/) meaning, *citizeness,* or else be accused of being against the Revolution.

The Art of the Revolution

The revolutionaries also encouraged new styles of art. They admired the civilizations of ancient Greece and Rome. They saw the ancient Greeks and Romans as models of modesty, **piety**, and devotion to duty. They contrasted these ancient virtues with those of the *ancien régime* aristocracy.

> **Vocabulary**
>
> **piety,** n. the quality of being deeply religious; the adherence to religious principles in daily life

Artists celebrated this theme in their paintings and sculptures. They painted contemporary figures in classical clothing and used figures and scenes from ancient times to make statements about contemporary events. Paintings usually focused on grand and heroic themes and told stories of noble events. The style was formal, with crisp outlines and cool colors.

This new **classicism**, or **neoclassicism**, was influenced and encouraged by the discovery and excavation of two ancient Roman cities. Herculaneum and Pompeii were buried in volcanic ash in the year 79 CE and rediscovered seventeen centuries later. Excavation of the two cities had begun in the mid-1700s. Images in neoclassical paintings often mimicked the actual pictures found on the walls of the excavated ruins.

> **Vocabulary**
>
> **classicism,** n. the ideas and styles found in the works of ancient Greece and Rome
>
> **neoclassicism,** n. a revival of ancient Greek and Roman ideas, especially in literature, art, or architecture

The most famous neoclassical artist of the Revolution was Jacques-Louis David (/zhahk/lwee/dah*veed/). David was also a member of the National Convention who voted for the death of the king. His painting, the *Tennis Court Oath,* emphasizes the heroism of the delegates who took an oath to never part until a constitution had been written.

Another of his works, *The Death of Marat,* shows one of the most famous events of the Revolution. Jean-Paul Marat was a radical journalist and a hero of the *sans culottes.* He was stabbed to death by a young woman as he was taking a bath. These paintings helped enflame the people with revolutionary fire.

In this painting, *The Death of Marat*, David painted the journalist Marat as a tragic hero of the Revolution.

Chapter 10
The Reign of Terror

The Revolution Turns Bloody When the French Revolution began in 1789, liberal-minded people throughout Europe and the United States applauded the change. Enlightenment ideals were being put into practice. People were beginning to throw off tyranny and live in liberty and justice.

The Big Question

What was the Reign of Terror?

By the end of 1793, the world was horrified by the savage turn the Revolution had taken. Nearly all the nations of Europe had lined up to fight a war against France. But the real savagery was about to begin.

Thousands of people were transported in tumbrels to their execution during the Reign of Terror.

The rumbling of the tumbrels, or carts, through the streets could be heard every afternoon. They carried the prisoners who had been convicted by the Revolutionary **Tribunal** that morning.

The tumbrels carried enemies of the Revolution. These might include a middle-aged woman whose crime was weeping as she watched her husband being guillotined, a young man who had chopped down a tree planted in honor of the Revolution, and a young woman who was rumored to have said she "did not care a fig" for the Revolution. If a person had a slip of the tongue and used *monsieur* or *madame,* that could be cause for becoming a "suspect."

Under the new **Law of Suspects**, anyone who criticized the Revolution in any way was possibly subject to trial and execution. How had it come to this?

The Jacobins and the Committee of Public Safety

When the Legislative Assembly took office in 1791, bourgeois citizens formed political clubs to discuss their ideas. Members were deputies of the Assembly. One of the most radical clubs was the **Jacobins**. When the National Convention took power, Jacobin leaders, along with the *sans culottes*, turned the Revolution on a violent path. It was the Jacobins who had demanded the deaths of Louis and Marie Antoinette. It was the Jacobins who had insisted on going to war against Austria and its allies. Many people, especially those in the countryside, disagreed with the Jacobins and the new path of the Revolution, and some were in open revolt. But the Jacobins soon took control of the government.

France was in serious trouble. Although there had been a few French successes in the war with Austria, things were going badly. The French army had suffered severe defeats. Enemy forces surrounded it, and a British fleet threatened coastal cities. In the countryside, there were uprisings and outright civil war in some provinces. What was worse, there were some people who were willing to welcome enemy troops. They were, for the most part, **royalists** and Catholics. Prices were rising, and food was in short supply. Many believed that the country was filled with **traitors** trying to overturn the Revolution. These people believed that the time had come for action.

To help solve these problems, the National Convention established the Committee of Public Safety. In July 1793, a man took control of the committee whose name has been associated with terror ever since.

Maximilien Robespierre

Was Maximilien Robespierre (/mak*see*mee*lyan /rohbz*pyair/) a man with high principles who worked tirelessly for the Revolution? Or was he a hypocrite a vain, self-centered, ruthless tyrant? His contemporaries could never agree, and historians have not settled the question either.

What is known is that he was a small man who rarely smiled. Green was his favorite color: even his eyeglasses were tinted green. He kept in his room a sculptured bust of himself, along with paintings and engravings showing him in various poses. By his bedside, he kept *Social Contract,* a book by Enlightenment

Robespierre remains a complex and controversial figure in French history. Although he supported the Reign of Terror, he was also known as the "Incorruptible" because he refused to take bribes or to profit from the Revolution.

philosopher Jean-Jacques Rousseau. He was completely dedicated to the Revolution.

Robespierre believed that he had to root out all opposition to the Revolution. Terror was his method and the motto of the Jacobins: "Let terror be the order of the day!" Terror, he claimed, would allow virtue to flourish.

In September 1793, the Committee of Public Safety introduced the Law of Suspects. Under it, people had only to be suspected of being a traitor—or of not wholeheartedly agreeing with the Revolution—to

The guillotine was an instrument of death and came to represent the horror of the Reign of Terror.

be brought to trial and condemned. They were brought by the thousands to the guillotine. On October 1, the prisons held 2,400 "suspects" awaiting trial and execution. By late December, they held 4,500. By the end of the Terror, people were being tried in groups of up to fifty at a time and sent to execution. The final death toll: about forty thousand French men and women were guillotined or shot.

The flow of blood, however, did not help the food shortage. In spite of controls put on the price of food, there was a near **famine** in Paris. On the base of the guillotine in the public square, some unknown graffiti artist wrote: "There is no butcher shop in Paris except upon this square!" It was fortunate for this man that Robespierre never found him, or he would have been executed next to his own graffiti.

> **Vocabulary**
>
> **famine,** n. an extreme shortage of food that results in widespread hunger

Robespierre's undoing came when he turned on fellow Jacobins in the National Convention. On July 27, 1794, Robespierre stood before a meeting of the convention. His purpose was to accuse several deputies of being suspects. But the deputies knew of his plans and had grown tired of the bloodletting.

Before he could speak, the deputies began shouting, "Down with the tyrant!" and "Long live the Republic!"

Robespierre and his friends on the Committee of Public Safety were taken to jail. Knowing that he was lost, Robespierre attempted to shoot himself, but he only wounded himself in the jaw. The next day, he too faced the guillotine, his face wrapped in bloody rags. Robespierre, the last leader of the Revolution, died in the same manner as those he had condemned.

The other committee members met the same fate. Among them was the young Saint-Just, the person who had insisted on the execution of Louis XVI. There was a terrible irony to these executions: the Revolution had spun so far out of control that the revolutionary leaders were now turning on each other.

In the end, Robespierre was taken to the guillotine, just like the thousands of people who had been sent to their death by him.

Chapter 11
Napoleon Bonaparte: Empire Builder

Emperor of the French It was the year 1804. A magnificent gilded coach pulled by eight horses with red leather harnesses arrived at the great Notre-Dame Cathedral. Two figures emerged. The beautiful woman wearing a sparkling diamond tiara entwined in her dark ringlets was Josephine.

The Big Question

What were the various reasons the people of France were willing to accept Napoleon as their emperor?

Her husband, Napoleon Bonaparte (/boh*nuh*part/), emerged behind her. He wore a white silk shirt and white breeches. Both wore long capes that spread out behind them like peacocks' tails.

Solemnly, Napoleon and Josephine marched down the center aisle of the cathedral, which was filled with eight thousand people shouting, "Long live the emperor!" The Catholic pope, Pius VII, conducted a ceremony, and Napoleon received the symbols of rulership—an orb, a sword, and a scepter.

Then Napoleon alone walked up the steps to the altar. He took the gold crown, shaped like the laurel wreaths awarded to ancient Roman heroes, and placed it on his own head. Josephine approached the altar, and as she knelt before him, Napoleon placed a crown on her head.

Napoleon crowned his wife, Josephine, empress.

Napoleon took the solemn oath: "I swear to uphold equality of rights and political and civil freedom. . . . I swear to rule for the interests, happiness, and glory of the people of France."

A herald announced, "The most glorious and most august [grand] Napoleon, emperor of the French, is consecrated [blessed] and enthroned!"

Napoleon was only thirty-two years old. He had already achieved enormous military success, and he would go on to become one of the great military geniuses in history. His **coronation** simply affirmed a role he had held since 1799—dictator of France.

How did France come such a long way—from the radical Reign of Terror to another single ruler—in so short a time?

The End of Terror

Do you remember when Robespierre and his radical supporters were overthrown in 1794? Everyone sighed with relief. Moderate bourgeois in the National Convention took control of the government. They passed a new constitution that gave control to a Directory of five members. But the new government faced the same old problems: food shortages, rising prices, and foreign wars.

In October 1795, royalists and *émigrés* felt the time was ripe to restore the *ancien régime.*

This painting by Antoine-Jean Gros, *Bonaparte at the Pont d'Arcole,* shows Napoleon as a fearless leader. Napoleon successfully led his troops against Austrian soldiers, defeating them at the Battle of Arcola in 1796.

Paris mobs attacked the Tuileries, where the National Convention was meeting. Napoleon, then twenty-six, was an officer in the French army. Called on to defend the convention, Napoleon ordered his troops to fire cannons point-blank into the crowd, killing and wounding hundreds. This "whiff of **grapeshot**," as it came to be called, put an end to the uprising and made Napoleon famous.

Napoleon had supported the Revolution. He had even joined the Jacobins. Then, in 1796, he was given command of the French forces. Napoleon was a brilliant military leader. He defeated several armies and increased France's territory. Napoleon intended to use his military successes to his advantage.

Napoleon Takes Control

Napoleon had always aspired to political power. By 1799, the people were losing faith in the Directory. They wanted strong leadership. It was an ideal moment for Napoleon to use his popularity to realize his dream of power.

On November 9, 1799, Napoleon made his move. He forced the five directors to resign. Then he forced the National Legislature to end the Directory and turn over the government to three consuls, of whom he was one. This marked the end of the French Revolution.

In 1800, the French overwhelmingly approved a new constitution that gave the real ruling power to Napoleon. He became Consul for Life in 1802. From then on, he had the power of a dictator.

But war still plagued France. They were fighting the British. Napoleon knew that France was tired of war. "Frenchmen," he proclaimed, "you want peace; your government wants it even more than you." But the British would not quit. King George III—the same king who had lost most of his American colonies to the American Revolution—was not willing to be humiliated by another revolutionary republican government. Furthermore, Britain

King George III was the British king who lost the American colonies.

feared France, and not just because of its armies. Britain was afraid that Enlightenment ideals would spread.

At first, King George's government refused to make peace. But after another Napoleon-led victory against the Austrians, the British decided they too were tired of war. In 1802, the British finally signed a peace treaty. After ten years of war and turmoil, Europe was at peace . . . at least for a while.

Bringing Order to France

After ten years of revolution and upheaval, people longed for stability. As soon as Napoleon took office, he began a series of reforms. He established a **national bank** and balanced the national budget, which stopped rising prices—people could now afford bread—and he also built roads and bridges.

<table>
<tr><td>

Vocabulary

national bank, n. a government bank that issues and manages a country's money
</td></tr>
</table>

One of Napoleon's most important reforms was his code of laws. Called the Napoleonic Code, these laws ensured several principles of the Revolution, including equality of male citizens before the law, the end of the Three Estates, and the right to own private property. People could also practice the religion of their choice. For women, however, the Code erased many of the rights they had won. Women were made dependents of their fathers or husbands. They were not independent citizens anymore. They could no longer own property. They could not file a lawsuit or act as a witness in court. If a married woman earned money, all of that money belonged to her husband. It was as though women were sent back to before the Revolution, while men moved forward.

In general, these changes appealed to the bourgeois and the peasants. Napoleon's success in governing, in addition to his military victories, made him seem irresistible.

When, in 1804, the question of making Napoleon emperor of the French was put to the people, they once again voted in his favor, although the voting was not free. After fifteen years of revolution and upheaval, France was once again under an absolute ruler.

The Grand Empire

Napoleon was one of history's military geniuses. As head of the French army from 1805 to 1809, he won battle after battle throughout Europe in his quest to build an empire—his desire for power was unlimited.

Each victory added more territory to his empire. He carved up pieces of Europe as gifts for his friends and relatives. His brother Joseph was made king of Naples and later king of Spain; his brother Louis became king of Holland;

Europe in 1810

Legend:
- French Empire
- Countries allied with Napoleon
- Countries controlled by Napoleon
- Countries at war with Napoleon

0 — 500 miles

N / W — E / S

60°N

Kingdom of Denmark and Norway

Sweden

Baltic Sea

United Kingdom of Great Britain and Ireland

North Sea

London

Brussels

Amiens

Versailles • Paris

ATLANTIC OCEAN

45°N

Loire River

Rhine River

French Empire

Elbe River

Prussia
Berlin

Warsaw

Russian Empire

Grand Duchy of Warsaw

Confederation of the Rhine

Prague
Vienna
Danube River

Austrian Empire

Helvetic Republic

Milan • Kingdom of Italy

Illyrian Provinces

Ottoman Empire

Black Sea

Po River

Marseille

Adriatic Sea

Portugal

Madrid

Barcelona

Corsica

Elba • Rome

Spain

Lisbon

Sardinia

Naples

Kingdom of Naples

Mediterranean Sea

0°

Sicily

15°E

Aegean Sea

15°W

By 1810, much of Europe was either directly or indirectly under Napoleon's control.

This cartoon from 1805 shows Napoleon and the British statesman, William Pitt, each carving out sections of a plum pie that resembles Earth.

and his brother Jerome was made king of Westphalia, in Germany. He gave his sister Elisa the Grand Duchy of Tuscany, in Italy. By 1810, much of Europe was either directly or indirectly under Napoleon's control. Russia and the Ottoman (or Turkish) Empire, remained outside his control.

A Disastrous Mistake

Napoleon's greatest mistake was invading Russia. In June 1812, he led a massive force of about six hundred thousand troops into Russia. Czar Alexander I of Russia knew his army couldn't beat Napoleon's forces and retreated. He withdrew his troops, who burned fields and slaughtered livestock, leaving nothing the French could use. French soldiers marched farther into Russia. In September, they reached Moscow and found it burning. Napoleon put out the fires and waited there for five weeks. The czar and his army just let him wait.

Then the French troops began their terrible winter retreat out of Russia. The army had entered Russia in June, in summer dress, with full bellies. But now no food remained, and the cold and snow delivered a terrible blow. Horses were the first to die, by the tens of thousands; in desperation, the men had no choice but to eat them. Without horses, the cavalry was on foot. Wagons and **artillery** were left by the road. Soon the men began to starve or freeze to death. Their

> ## Vocabulary
>
> **artillery,** n. large guns that are used to shoot across long distances
>
> **Cossacks,** n. soldiers from southwestern Russia, known for their skills on horseback

boots worn out, they wrapped their feet in rags, leaving bloody footprints in the snow. Then the Russian fighters appeared. Mounted troops known as **Cossacks** attacked and killed the retreating French. This was one of history's greatest military disasters. Of the six hundred thousand men who left for Russia, only thirty thousand returned to their homelands. Napoleon's power was weakened, and his enemies took advantage.

Napoleon's invasion of Russia was a disaster. This painting, known as *Retreat from Russia,* by Nicolas Toussaint Charlet, shows the horror of what the French soldiers experienced.

The ultimate humiliation came in 1814, when enemy armies marched into Paris and occupied the city. Defeated, Napoleon gave up his throne and was **exiled** to Elba, a small island off the coast of Italy. The brother of the executed Louis XVI was installed as King Louis XVIII of France.

Return from Exile

Napoleon escaped from Elba a few months later. On March 1, he landed on the shores of France, near Marseilles (/mar*se*yuh/), with about one thousand men and began the march to Paris. Along the way, he was greeted by people who remembered France's days of glory and were already tired of Louis XVIII.

Napoleon faced little resistance when he escaped from Elba and returned to Paris on March 20, 1815.

Royal troops had been ordered to stop Napoleon. As Napoleon approached the troops, his own soldiers' band played "The Marseillaise," the stirring song of the Revolution, which had been outlawed by the new king. Napoleon dismounted and walked toward the line of seven hundred men; all had their muskets raised. The commander of the royal troops shouted to his men, "There he is! Fire!"

Napoleon stopped and flung his arms wide. "If you want to kill your emperor," he called to the men, "here I am." He held his breath. But instead, a great shout arose: "Long live the emperor!"

Napoleon met no more resistance. Louis XVIII fled Paris when he heard the news, and an alarmed Europe quickly organized its armies.

Waterloo

In Paris, Napoleon easily took control of the government and rebuilt an army. On June 12, he left Paris for his last battle.

The battle took place on June 18, 1815, near Waterloo, in present-day Belgium. It had rained the night before the battle. The downpour was so heavy that Napoleon was forced to delay his plan to open battle at 6:00 a.m. The ground was too muddy for horses and artillery to move about, so Napoleon had to wait for it to dry out.

Napoleon proudly surveyed his troops. His army numbered about seventy-four thousand; his opponent, the British military hero, the Duke of Wellington, commanded almost as many soldiers. Despite the evenly matched forces, Napoleon was confident that this would be an easy victory.

At 11:30 a.m., the French began to move, and a fierce battle erupted. The fighting was bloody and punctuated with the roar of cannons. It continued through the long afternoon.

The battle of Waterloo, where Napoleon was defeated by the Duke of Wellington, is one of the most famous battles in history. In the center of this painting, you can see the Duke of Wellington urging his soldiers on.

At 4:30 p.m., fifty thousand Prussian troops arrived and reinforced Wellington's attack. The battlefield became soaked with blood as horses and troops who fought all day lay dead and dying. Napoleon tried but failed to rally his troops; he was overwhelmed and suffered a crushing defeat. Wellington lost about one-quarter of his forces. Of the seventy-four thousand troops Napoleon commanded that day at Waterloo, almost half lay dead or wounded.

Napoleon's final attempt at power had failed. He was exiled to the distant island of St. Helena off the coast of Africa, where he eventually died.

An era had ended. The French Revolution and the era of Napoleon had a dramatic effect on Europe and the world. The world had witnessed one of the bloodiest revolutions in history, a revolution that resulted in the fall of the French monarchy and the rise of the middle class. Napoleon's armies had carried many of the ideas of the French Revolution throughout Europe during his quest for empire. The 1800s would be marked by a series of revolutions as the ideals of liberty and equality spread to old and new nations.

Chapter 12
The Romantic Revolution

A Cultural Movement The French Revolution and the rise and fall of Napoleon changed the way people thought, not only about politics and religion but also about literature and the arts. You have already read about one artistic movement that grew out of the French Revolution—the neoclassicism of Jacques-Louis David.

The Big Question

What were the differences between the Neoclassical and the Romantic artists, and how were those differences reflected in their work?

In this chapter, you will learn about another important movement that was spurred by the French Revolution but that defined itself in opposition to neoclassicism—the Romantic movement.

Rousseau and Native Americans

One of the fathers of the Romantic movement was Jean-Jacques Rousseau (/zhahn/zhack/rooh*soh/). He was the philosopher who complained that, "Man is born free and everywhere he is in chains." That line helped spark the French Revolution. But there was more to Rousseau than just this one line.

Rousseau was also famous for claiming that human beings are born good but are made worse by civilization and society. In the 1700s, this was a truly shocking idea. At that time, everyone assumed that civilization and society were good and

In addition to the French Revolution, the writings of Jean-Jacques Rousseau helped inspire the Romantic movement.

necessary things. The French aristocrats and philosophers were certain that it was good to be "civilized" and bad to be "uncivilized."

Rousseau disagreed. He thought that being civilized and living in modern society did people more harm than good. Rousseau admired the Native Americans of North America. He believed that because of their social structure and lack of emphasis on material possessions, they were better able to appreciate important things such as nature, family ties, and they directly benefited from hard work.

At the time, very few people agreed with Rousseau's ideas. Still, he chose to live his life in accordance with his ideas. He spent a great deal of time by himself, going on long walks, appreciating the beauties of nature, and exploring his own emotions and imagination. Although his books were widely attacked, they influenced a whole generation of Romantic writers, painters, and musicians.

Neoclassicism and Romanticism

Just as Rousseau and the French revolutionaries sought changes and reform of the "old" ideas and the "old" ways, so too did the Romantic artists of the late 1700s and early 1800s. These artists rebelled against the accepted artistic ideas of their day. In particular, they rebelled against the ideas of neoclassicism.

Neoclassical artists believed that the way to make great art was to study the works of the ancient Greeks and Romans and then imitate those works. The Romantics were less interested in imitation and more interested in originality and "doing their own thing."

Neoclassical artists believed that artists should confine themselves to subjects such as heroes or leaders, and treat those subjects with great seriousness and dignity. The Romantics were more interested in everyday subjects and wrote about them in a simpler style.

Neoclassical artists were heavily influenced by the ideas of the Enlightenment. They valued thought, reason, and the life of the mind. The Romantics were certainly not opposed to thinking, but they placed more emphasis on feeling.

Here you can see a neoclassical painting of a young Napoleon Bonaparte by the French painter Jean-Auguste-Dominique Ingres.

This is a painting of Polish composer Frédéric Chopin, also of the Romantic era, by the French Romantic painter Eugène Delacroix.

Neoclassical artists valued order. Whether they were creating poems, paintings, or **symphonies**, they wanted everything to be arranged in a very orderly and systematic way. Romantic artists generally placed less emphasis on order and more emphasis on creativity and spontaneity.

Three Romantic Artists

After the French Revolution, a generation of European artists embraced Romantic ideas. One of the most characteristic of these Romantic artists was the English poet William Wordsworth (1770–1850).

Wordsworth wrote poems about normal, everyday people, including peasants and beggars. He didn't use fancy words and poetic phrases. Instead, he tried to use language that was more like the language spoken by real men and women. He also tried to bring emotions and feelings into his poems. Wordsworth believed that good poetry is "the spontaneous overflow of powerful feelings."

Although Wordsworth himself read a lot, his poems urged his readers to set aside their books and experience nature. In one poem, he suggested that a person could learn more about life by walking in the woods on a spring day than by reading all the books ever written.

Wordsworth based many of his poems on things he saw on his walks in the woods. For example, he describes how he saw a field of daffodils that seemed to be dancing gleefully beside a lake. In the poem, Wordsworth not only describes daffodils, he also describes his feelings about seeing the daffodils. At the end of the poem, he says that he often thinks back to the day when he saw the dancing flowers. "And then," Wordsworth writes, "my heart with pleasure fills, / And dances with the daffodils."

Wordsworth also wrote poems about children. He admired children for the same reason that Rousseau admired Native Americans. Wordsworth believed children were more natural and less **corrupted** by civilization.

> **Vocabulary**
> ----
> **corrupt,** v. to harm or to contaminate

I WANDERED LONELY AS A CLOUD

I wandered lonely as a cloud

That floats on high o'er vales and hills,

When all at once I saw a crowd,

A host, of golden daffodils;

Beside the lake, beneath the trees,

Fluttering and dancing in the breeze.

This is the first stanza of a famous poem Wordsworth wrote around 1804.

Wordsworth was in France during the early years of the French Revolution. He was very excited about what was happening there. He could see that the old rules were being thrown away. He felt optimistic that the Revolution would bring about a better world. When the Revolution turned violent however, Wordsworth changed his mind. But he still believed in the ideas that had inspired the French Revolution.

England produced a number of Romantic painters too. One of the best known of these painters was John Constable (1776–1837). Constable is sometimes called "the Wordsworth of painting." Just as Wordsworth tried to capture the beauties of nature in his poems, Constable tried to capture them in landscape paintings. Constable loved to walk the roads and paths near his home. He studied the shapes and colors of rivers, fields, hillsides, and haystacks. Constable wanted his paintings to be realistic and to convey feelings and emotions. "Painting," he once said, "is but another word for feeling."

This John Constable painting is titled *Salisbury Cathedral from the Meadows.*

Of the many Romantic composers, perhaps the best known is German composer Ludwig van Beethoven (/bay*toh*ven/) (1770–1827). Beethoven, trained as a classical musician, learned to play in a very orderly and elegant manner. As he grew older, both his musical compositions and his playing style became more energetic. Beethoven was a man of dramatic emotions, and he was able to use music to convey his emotions to his audiences. A contemporary noted that when Beethoven played sad music, his audiences often began weeping. On the other hand, when he played happy music, people stomped their feet, applauded loudly, and waved their hats in the air!

Like other Romantic artists, Beethoven was a great walker and lover of nature. He went for a walk almost every day. He once boasted, "No one can love the country as much as I do." Once Beethoven even turned his walking experiences into a symphony, sometimes called the "Pastoral Symphony." In this symphony, he used various instruments to capture the sounds of nature.

Beethoven sympathized with the goals of the French Revolution and admired Napoleon—at first. The German composer even wrote a symphony, sometimes called the "Heroic Symphony," dedicated to the French general. However, when Napoleon crowned himself emperor, Beethoven became angry and tore up the dedication to Napoleon. Beethoven, like so many Romantic artists, felt that Napoleon had betrayed the ideals of the French Revolution by becoming just another tyrant.

The Legacy of Romanticism

Romanticism still exists today. People still listen to Beethoven's music, look at Constable's paintings, and read Wordsworth's poems. Romanticism is also with us as an idea, or set of ideas, that many of us take for granted. Whenever we wish we could go back to the pure and simple days of childhood, whenever we praise someone for showing creativity, go for a walk in the woods, or pour out our innermost feelings in a diary, we are acting in accordance with the Romantic ideas that were developed during the era of the French Revolution.

Ludwig van Beethoven is considered one of the greatest composers of all time.

Glossary

A

"absolute monarch," (phrase) a king or queen who has the unchecked authority to do whatever he or she wants without any restrictions (60)

archive, n. a place where public records or historical documents are kept (107)

arrogance, n. a belief or feeling of superiority (91)

artillery, n. large guns that are used to shoot across long distances (147)

B

bourgeois, n. the wealthy members of French society, such as landlords, who were also part of the Third Estate; people who were neither nobles or peasants (72)

C

cathedral, n. the bishop's church; any large and important church (128)

censor, v. to remove or prohibit books, art, films, or other media that the government finds offensive, immoral, or harmful (61)

"citizens' militia," (phrase) an army composed of the people of a nation rather than of soldiers (112)

civic, adj. relating to a city, citizen, or community (128)

classicism, n. the ideas and styles found in the works of ancient Greece and Rome (132)

constitutional monarchy, n. government by a king or queen whose power is limited by a constitution (115)

coronation, n. the ceremony or act of crowning a ruler (142)

corrupt, v. to harm or to contaminate (156)

Cossacks, n. soldiers from southwestern Russia, known for their skills on horseback (147)

courtier, n. a person who serves as a friend or adviser to a ruler in his or her court (76)

D

dauphin, n. the title given to the prince who is next in line to inherit the French throne (84)

delegation, n. a group of people chosen to speak on behalf of a larger group (97)

despotism, n. tyranny; rule by a leader who has total and often oppressive power (123)

"divine right of kings," (phrase) the belief that kings and queens have a God-given right to rule, and that rebellion against them is a sin (63)

duke, n. a male noble who rules a small territory (78)

E

Estates-General, n. an assembly made up of representatives from France's Three Estates (94)

exile, v. to to force someone to live outside of a place as a punishment (148)

F

famine, n. an extreme shortage of food that results in widespread hunger (138)

feudal, adj. relating to the medieval system of exchanging land for service and loyalty (71)

"finance minister," (phrase) the government official in charge of a country's money (102)

"foreign ambassador," (phrase) a person from another country who is an official representative of his or her government (88)

G

grapeshot, n. a small mass of metal balls packed into a canvas bag, resembling a cluster of grapes, that is shot from a cannon (143)

guillotine, n. a machine designed to behead people quickly and with little pain (123)

I

indulge, v. to allow someone to do what they want; to spoil someone (84)

interest, n. the money paid by a borrower for the use of someone else's money (94)

J

Jacobin, n. a member of a violent, extreme left-wing group during the French Revolution (136)

L

Law of Suspects, n. a law passed during the French Revolution that allowed the arrest of people suspected of opposing the Revolution (136)

Legislative Assembly, n. a group of representatives with the power to make laws for the country (118)

N

national bank, n. a government bank that issues and manages a country's money (145)

natural law, n. a system of rights or justice that is shared by all people and that comes from nature, not the rules of society (110)

neoclassicism, n. a revival of ancient Greek and Roman ideas, especially in literature, art, or architecture (132)

P

"parish priest," (phrase) a person in a local church who has the training or authority to carry out certain religious ceremonies or rituals (70)

piety, n. the quality of being deeply religious; the adherence to religious principles in daily life (131)

province, n. an area or region similar to a state (107)

R

reform, n. an improvement (62)

regime, n. a period of rule (70)

reign, v. to rule over a country as its czar, king, or queen (76)

republic, n. a government in which people elect representatives to rule for them (118)

royalist, n. a supporter of the king or queen (137)

S

symphony, n. a musical composition written for an orchestra and usually in four parts called movements (155)

T

Third Estate, n. in France, everyone who was not a member of the nobility or clergy; included everyone from the poorest of the poor to the wealthy middle class (71)

tithe, n. one-tenth of a person's income, paid to support a church (70)

title deed, n. a document stating a person's legal ownership (107)

traitor, n. a person who is disloyal; a person who betrays his or her country (137)

treasury, n. a place where money and other riches of a government are kept (67)

tribunal, n. a type of court; a group appointed to make judgments (136)

tyrannical, adj. characteristic of a tyrant or tyranny; cruel or unjust (64)

Y

yoke, n. a harness used to restrain work animals; something that takes away people's freedom (107)

CKHG™
Core Knowledge HISTORY AND GEOGRAPHY™

Editorial Directors
Linda Bevilacqua and Rosie McCormick

The Enlightenment
Subject Matter Expert

Mark G. Spencer, PhD, Department of History, Brock University

Illustration and Photo Credits

The French Revolution and Romanticism
Subject Matter Expert
Mary K. Gayne, PhD, Department of History, James Madison University

Illustration and Photo Credits